# AFTER
# the
# MUD

## Stories of the
## U.S. NAVY and WORLD WAR II

*To Bud,*

*enjoy*

*Biel Shrunt*
*5/12/07*

# AFTER
# the
# MUD

### Stories of the
### U.S. NAVY and WORLD WAR II

## Bill Shrout

ħbp

HONEYBIL PUBLISHING

P.O. BOX 2806
CLACKAMAS, OR. 97015

*Dedicated:*

> *First*
>
> To my parents and my home town community for instilling in me the real values of life. With them I was able to cope with the world I found outside of Akron.
>
> *Second*
>
> To Captain (Skipper) Carlton and the crew of the **73.** Without their watchful eye and attentiveness to our environment, I might not have been here to tell this story.
>
> *and Thirdly*
>
> To my wife, Julie, and our three children, Linda, Terry and Rick, for their loving encouragement and assistance in the book's completion.

# CONTENTS

To Order Additional Copies of:

## AFTER THE MUD

Sent postpaid @ $18.00 each


Other books by Bill Shrout:
*FROM MUD PIES and LILAC LEAVES*
*hardback edition*

*Sent postpaid @ $20.00 each*

*Make Checks Payable in U.S. Funds to:*
*Honeybil Publishing*
*P.O. Box 2806*
*Clackamas, OR 97015*

# PROLOGUE

It seems like only yesterday that I bid my fellow high school classmates good-by. We had gathered in the heart of Akron at its main watering hole, the Eat Rite Cafe. Akron is a small town in North Central Indiana that pleasures the near-by inhabitants with the opportunity of securing gas, groceries, dry goods, and in the case of the Eat Rite Cafe, hamburgers, pie, coke and coffee.

Akron High School had bid its thirty-four graduates farewell on this warm evening in April, 1944, and I was one of those excited graduates. I shall endeavor to tell you, the reader, what it was like to come of age in a time our country faced its biggest challenge, World War II. I will attempt to relay the feelings of a young man, fresh from farm life and the gentle cover of his mother's love and wisdom. I hope the reader will be able to sense the built in security of my caring friends and neighbors as I was quickly thrust into the routines and expectations of the world outside of the Akron community.

1

## SHROUT - AFTER the MUD

World War ll was big time and everyone had a brother, or in some cases more than one, already in some branch of the service. War was on all of our minds. We did not have access to newspapers or television as we have today. The absence of the media did not hamper our understanding of what was happening in the world about us. Almost everyone had images implanted in their minds of how horrible the war must be, as it was referred to "over across the pond." The hardships that our servicemen were going through became fixations that permeated the deepest crevices of our thinking. My memory was etched forever with the reality of the world situation.

*After the Mud* was written as a sequel to *From Mud Pies and Lilac Leaves,* a story of the author's early years. One will read how decades later the vivid remembrances live on. The author recalls the processes of enlisting, boot camp and the endless days of bobbing up and down like a cork as he rode his ship of war into harm's way.

Most shipmates' names will be real. Some will be changed in order to tell the story without offending. Some phrases and words that may be offensive in today's society, were acceptable and commonly used in the 1940's. The intent of this book is to be accurate to the times of that day. The dates are exact along with other pertinent information that could only come from a ship's deck log.

# 1

# WORK OR WAR

## School is Out

It was a happy bunch that met down at the "Eat Rite" after the graduation of the AHS class of "44." The air was full of, "What are you going to do?" Crazy expectations of the future were flowing all over the place. A person would have thought that each of the graduates was at least thirty years old. The young men in my class all knew that they would have to obtain some fast military training and then start killing the enemy. Since some were sons of farmers, they might be able to get a farm deferment. Most did not want to talk about deferment, but it was happening in a few instances. Some would find out that they could not pass the physical exam. All of this maneuvering of the mind seemed to add years to our young and short on experience lives.

I was seventeen years old. Already I was starting to take on the feeling of having no fear. It seemed right to be thinking of defending our country. Equally as strong as the Christian principles that I embraced, was the belief that the United States of America was the most perfect country on the face of the earth. The thoughts of my mind ran parallel with my nation's conviction that Germany and Japan had to be stopped and put in their place. It was common to listen in on the downtown curbside conversations and hear expressions like, "Just get me over there and boy, wouldn't I get me a few Japs and Krouts!" I knew that I was emotionally getting myself in position to do just about any command given to me if and when I made it to the front line.

Many of the front windows of the homes in the Akron area displayed service flags, bearing a blue star for each person in the military service from that house. It was not uncommon to see windows that were dressed with flags containing three and sometimes four stars. The unfortunate homes that had a gold star on their flag signified that a son or daughter had paid with their life in defense of their country. We would hear of a family's loss and although sincerely sorry for their misfortune, knew that this tragedy and many more would have to be in order to save our democracy.

When I graduated from high school, our house had a flag with one blue star in honor of my brother, Adrian. He was a member of the Army Air Force. I would write letters to him and include within them expressions of how I would soon be joining him in some sort of battle. I would say things like, "Keep them flying, cause I'm coming!" For a time I thought that I would probably enlist in the Army Air Force. I was proud of my brother and felt within my heart that I, too, must represent our family and defend this wonderful nation where we were so privileged to live.

Soon there would be another blue star added to the flag that Mom and Dad so proudly displayed in our front window. Not many people passed our farm house, since it was situated on a dirt road. But Dad was proud. He could not go himself, but he was content in knowing that his sons could go, and in a way, represent him in this hour of our country's need.

Thirty-four seniors had made it through all of the rigors and requirements that the State of Indiana had put upon them to be eligible to receive an official high school diploma. It was now their turn to face reality. Life was at a check point. "Man, it sure is great to be an adult," surged through each of the graduates' thoughts. As I slowly devoured a wedge of chocolate pie that the Eat Rite was famous for, I was hit with the sharp reality that as an adult I was soon going to be required to do my part in the combat war effort. It was very difficult to savor all of the pie's excellent flavor and have such heavy thoughts on my mind. I knew that I would soon be drafted into the military. I also knew that I wanted to be able to pick the branch in which I wanted to serve. It seemed so correct to think this way. I could almost hear the Navy marching bands playing "Anchors Aweigh," just like it sounded on the radio from Station WOWO in Fort Wayne or Station WIBC in Indianapolis. Many of the radio stations that came in plain enough to hear, would play the Navy Anthem and other military service anthems on a regular basis. I could feel my allegiance changing from the Army Air Force to the U.S. Navy. It must have been the band music.

The prevailing mood of wanting to serve one's country was fueled mostly by the small talk between neighbors. Sometimes a neighbor would stop along beside the highway for a chat on his way home from a trip into Akron. He perhaps had found or heard some new piece of information. Not all homes took a daily newspaper. Some would hear something new and would use the party line telephone to pass on the news. It was considered to be an okay thing to listen in or "eaves drop."

Since I was only seventeen it was necessary to get my parents' permission to join whatever branch that I might select. I believed that Dad and Mom would sign for me. My parents were as patriotic as anyone. They knew that "Ol' Hitler" and the "Japs" had to be stopped. Young men all across the country were enlisting right and left into the armed forces. There never was a thought not to serve. The nation had only one major assignment in its immediate focus. There were no peace demonstrations, no talk about "What are we doing there?" Everyone was saying, "Let's win the war!" It was so natural for me and my friends to have our country's need of our assistance saturated throughout our entire being.

Current war news was almost impossible to come by in the small town community of Akron. True, we were emerging from the Great Depression. Two and one-half years of World War II had paved the way for a much improved economic status throughout the country. If anyone wanted work, there were many jobs begging for someone to take. Making planes and tanks and building bombs were top priority. Factories making all of this necessary war equipment and supplies were running day and night, seven days a week. Women in America were assuming new responsibilities. They were becoming a major work force in our country's defense. It was difficult for local farmers to get the extra help they needed to take care of tending and harvesting crops. In some cases, the vacancy created by someone's son enlisting in the service created a true hardship. It was difficult for some fathers to convince their sons to stay home and help with the raising of food for the armed forces.

When a teenage farm boy finished high school, he had to make the important decision of whether he was going to try to get a deferment from serving in the military. If he were a son of a farmer who had a farm of some size he could usually find a way to convince the draft board that he should stay home and help his dad with the farm. But patriotism was very prevalent. It was always demonstrating itself from almost every street corner, even in small towns like Akron that had a limited number of corners. It became a matter of pride to most. Military service was the only way for many to express their feelings for what had happened to America.

I would learn the latest war news from someone who had a working radio or had access to a daily paper. We would stand or sit around the downtown square of Akron, swapping whatever we knew or thought we knew. The Eat Rite had a natural place for us to sit, a built-in curb in front of the big, plate glass window. Most evenings in good weather you could count on finding several of the town's most eligible military bound young males sitting there. When the weather did not cooperate with the use of the exterior built-in bench, we would adjourn to the inside of the cafe.

I was a sophomore in high school when the Japanese attacked Pearl Harbor. During the next two and one-half years, until I graduated, I had many opportunities

8

to swap small talk about the current world situation. I spent many hours in downtown Akron discussing the world events and the future of our great country. Our inspirations were not fueled by television anchors and the consistent bombardment of television cable talk shows that are prevalent at the time of this writing. We made our decisions pure and simple--no one to lure us into their way of thinking. Our training and upbringing came to the forefront. We instinctively knew what was the right and correct thing to do, and we were determined to do just that.

Just before Christmas in my senior year of high school, Dad and Mom bought forty acres about three-quarters of a mile east of Akron. This was an important assist to my driving to town, the "ol' thirty-three" with the "A" gas rationing stamp on the upper right hand side of its windshield. I did not need as much gasoline as I did commuting from the Shewman farm, where I had lived. Therefore I could be in Akron in the discussion of current affairs on a more regular basis. I finished school commuting by hack (school bus) to Akron High.

## The Start of the Real World

One of my high school teachers, George Cullers, had found summer employment at General Tire & Rubber Company in Wabash. Wabash is about twenty-five miles south and east of where we lived. The nostalgia of this small city was enhanced in the writing of the now world famous state song of Indiana. The river that meanders through, making river banks in this North Central Indiana town, carries the same name as the small town of Wabash it transverses.

I decided to apply at General Tire for a job. I was easily accepted. If you were over sixteen years old, warm and breathing, you made it. I started working on the early evening shift because of my need for transportation and that was when I could get a ride to work. My teacher friend agreed to pick me up at the farm, take me to work and deliver me home for fifty cents per day. I thought that was a good deal and I took him up on it.

I started working at General Tire in the recap department. Most of the plant's efforts and energies were consumed in war products. A part of the overall national war effort was to conserve rubber and particularly in auto

10

tires. Recapping a tire was the first alternative. I worked at several tasks in this department. Sometimes I was assigned to working the "belt." The rubber would be extruded through a mill and would lead out onto a long moving conveyor belt. The rubber was very hot coming from the mill and needed some cooling time. As the continuous strip of recapping moved down the belt it became cooled by air exposure and by some cool water being sprayed upon it.

About fifty feet down the belt, another worker and I would take turns cutting a two inch sample strip from a long continuous strip as it approached the winder. The sample was for testing and was marked for that particular run. When it was my turn to do the sample cutting, my belt buddy would grab the loose end after I had taken the sample and would start it onto the winder. We would repeat this throughout the remainder of the shift.

Another assignment I had was to run the slitter machine. A slitter cut the material into various widths, then laminated it to the recap strip as it was rolled up. This kept the rubber recap strip from sticking together.

It was very hot working in the plant, even at night. I would race with other workers on how many cokes we could drink and then lineup the empty bottles in our work area to demonstrate our holding capacity. All of this was a new experience for me. I found while working in the rough and tough work place that I was learning how to goof off and only do what little you could get away with. This really went against the grain. I was taught differently. Dad always said, "Do a good days work for your pay." Oh well, I was now introduced to the big bad world. Little did I know of what was around the corner of life for the little farm boy from Akron.

## Look Out, Hitler!

Night after night I would make the trip to Wabash and do my thing in the recap department of General Tire. I found myself pondering the idea of enlisting in some branch of the service. I found myself still making the short trip into Akron and talking with anyone I could find who wanted to talk about the war.

Enough was enough! I decided to go down to Indianapolis by bus around the first part of May and try to enlist in The U.S. Coast Guard. When I got there, they were not taking any new recruits. A Navy recruiter nearby, who heard what the Coast Guard told me, said they would be glad to have me join the U.S. Navy. I picked up the handouts that he offered and I went back to Akron by bus. The Navy seemed to be about the same as the Coast Guard to this farm boy. The pictures of their uniforms looked about the same, and after all, water is water and ships are ships. I started thinking Navy.

June and July still found me working evenings at General Tire. I was sleeping most of the day and wondering if this was what I really wanted to do. I kept thinking about the service and if I should just go ahead and enlist. After much soul searching, I found myself going down to Kokomo. I signed up with the Navy recruiter. This action took place on July 8, 1944. The recruiting office told me to go home and wait for a date to take the physical examination. Since I was under twenty-one years of age, I had to get Dad's and Mom's signatures on the permission slip. I discussed this in some length with my parents and without too much reluctance, they signed it. I sent it back to the recruiter and waited.

Sure enough, the time went very quickly. On the 28th day of July, 1944, the all-expectant letter arrived. Bright and early on the morning of July 31, Dad drove me to Peru, some 30 miles south of Akron, to catch a bus. Normally I would have boarded the bus in Akron, but we had missed the Akron to Peru bus. I was able to catch another in Peru that had come from some other town.

I know Dad did not feel too good about seeing his youngest leave. But Dad was the type that was proud of the military and what it stood for. He had one son in the service and now another one about to go in. I recall in growing up, Dad would tell me stories his dad had told him about serving in the Civil War under General Humphrey Marshall. Dad would just add another blue star to the service flag that was displayed so proudly in the living room front window. Only neighbors going back and forth on the narrow dirt road to Akron would see the flag. But that was all right with Dad. He made his statement to the world the best way he knew, of how he felt about living in America.

During my lifetime, shopping experiences in cities larger than Akron were few in number. Akron shopping and securing my education within its borders was hardly ever more complicated than two cars at the one and only crossroad in the center of town, vying for traffic rights. In my earlier recollection, there might have been a horse drawn wagon or two getting into trouble. Life in Akron was simple and the word stress had not made much headway in the vocabulary of our small community.

My folks might go once a year to Warsaw, a county seat in the next county to our north. I longed for Dad to go a little out of his way and give me a chance to perhaps catch a peek at one of the many big lakes in or around Warsaw. I always kept hoping for the need of that special purchase that would have to be made in Warsaw. I remember one time Mom purchasing a piece of linoleum carpet all rolled up in a nice tight roll to put on the rough kitchen floor at the Shewman farm. This farm was home to me for my first seventeen years. The carpet purchase had to be made in Warsaw. Mom thought she needed more to chose from than the only two available at Dan Leininger and Sons General Mercantile Store in Akron.

Rochester was our county seat and was just eleven miles west of Akron. Dad would go there for license plates for the family car and any other county paperwork that he might need. I do not remember purchasing any items in Rochester, just going there for car license plates. When I was sixteen, I made the trip and acquired my driving license. At most, a Rochester trip was only needed two or three times a year.

Dan Leininger & Sons General Mercantile, the principle store in Akron, did not carry everything, even though it might appear to me that it did. As a young farm boy growing up near Akron and wandering about this "big" store, I was constantly amazed with all of the different items and gadgets that were on display. I wondered how it was that someone had thought up all of those nice inventions and found a way to market them. Leiningers tried very hard to keep us from having to shop anywhere else. They managed to help keep the trips out of town to the bigger stores few and far between.

15

My growing up experiences and minimal exposure to large city life were about to be quickly put to the test. I was to be thrust into a new world, a world that I had heard very little about and certainly did not know what to expect. When I arrived on the bus in Indianapolis, all of the heavy duty traffic and the hum and noise of the big city's daily business happenings were overwhelming. I quickly decided I really wanted to go back to the farm. Down-town Akron was certainly not anything like this. I told myself that I was here to take a physical and get myself ready to go into Uncle Sam's Navy. Bravely, I left the bus at the bus station and walked to the Navy recruiter's office located close by. My heart was really pounding. All of the necessary paperwork had been turned in and all I had to do now to be in Uncle Sam's Navy was to pass the physical. Wow! I was really pumped! I was ready for come what may.

As I looked around the recruiter's office, I observed other farm-looking young men. Even I could tell some of them looked different. We farm boys kind of stood out. I was also quick to note that some of the recruits had a different sound. As soon as I heard them talk and brag about this and that, I knew they must be city guys. They loaded all of us, city and farm alike, onto Navy buses and took us somewhere. To this day, I can not place where we went to take the physical, but I remember it was a short bus ride.

The big mix of social backgrounds had begun. From that day forward, little Billy would never be the same. I was to find that even though I would try my best to keep my mother's philosophies  and teachings close in my thoughts, I would be tested. I believe that I was starting to come out of the shell that living so close to the farm had created. The war, and the gasoline rationing it fostered, played a significant role in discouraging unnecessary travel. I did not go many places during the first dozen years of life. The shell of self protection and farm security  showed evidences of hairline cracks as I ventured out into the world about me.

One thing that stands out in my memory is seeing all of the naked men standing around waiting to be examined and approved for entry into the United States Navy. I grew up in an environment that did not encourage parading around in one's birthday suit.  It is true, I would see a dozen or so male students showering after a high school physical education class or after basketball practice and games.  But I knew all of those guys, and besides, we quickly showered and got dressed.   Here, to this little farm boy, were what  looked like  thousands (must have been at least hundreds) of naked guys, all standing around trying to look casual and as if this was something they did every day.  I did not know any of them.  They were all strangers. What I was made to take part in was not normal to me and made me feel very uncomfortable.

# SHROUT - AFTER the MUD

The line of men moved ever so slowly from one doctor to the next. Some of the doctors were in little rooms with no doors, about twelve feet square. Others sat at small desks or tables in the larger areas of the hall that we were proceeding down. Each progression meant one more step for each of us in the process of becoming a sailor.

Somewhere in this slow moving line, my heart almost did a flip. A couple female nurses came strolling by just as casual as you please. We did not have a thing to cover up with. I was mortified. The nurses appeared to not be in a hurry and seemed to be enjoying their assignment. They smiled and looked us up and down as they leisurely strolled by. Not since my mother had bathed me as a little boy had any female gazed at my fully exposed body.

The experiences of this day would be the beginning of my dropping the barriers of modesty that I had clutched so closely about myself while living the good farm life. I was in a new age. The world outside of Akron and my beloved Shewman farm was engulfing me and doing it much faster than I wanted it to. I quickly told myself that I must adjust. This was the way it was going to be and I had better just get used to it.

Just before the break for lunch (to me it had always been dinner), I remember this incident. A young man in front of me was five pounds short of the minimum Navy admittance requirement. The person weighing him told him to eat as many bananas as he could during the lunch break. And he did just that. I saw him later in the line that afternoon. He told me he had purchased ten pounds of bananas, ate most of them, and managed to meet the weight requirements. I asked him how he felt. He told me not bad, just a little full and he did not think he would eat another banana for quite a while. I guess bananas are the easiest thing to eat a lot of and retain the weight when you are attempting to do what he was trying to do.

The line past the many Navy doctors continued throughout the afternoon. I thought to myself that I sure was glad it was summertime. The building might not have been too warm in the middle of the winter to parade around naked. About four o'clock we finished. Was I ever thrilled! I had accomplished what I had come to Indianapolis to do. I had passed! I was told to come back for the swearing in ceremony the next morning on the steps of the Soldier's and Sailor's Monument, a landmark of downtown Indianapolis.

My brother, Irvin, and his wife, Dorothy, lived in Indianapolis, where he was a student at Butler University. I called him and he came downtown and picked me up. I stayed with them in their apartment that evening. He returned me to the Soldier's and Sailor's Monument the next morning. It was the Navy's practice at that time to

19

have the Navy Band as part of the swearing in ceremony. Many times I had heard the swearing in procedure broadcast over WIBC Radio. Now I was to be a part of that inspiring tradition that had caused my heart to skip a beat! This was an exciting time!

The Navy band played several inspiring Sousa marches as we waited around with much anticipation to what was immediately ahead of us. Then the exciting moment came. With tremendous pride in our voices, we joined in one loud voice, each inserting our own full name at the proper place, and then swearing to honorably defend to death our beautiful country. At that moment we became the latest group of young Americans to be sworn into the United States Navy. What a beautiful sunny Indiana August morning for this memorable service to take place. I felt like taking the steps two at a time as I bounced down them to the waiting Navy bus.

After the conclusion of the swearing in ceremony, we had been told to go home and we would be notified when to come back to Indianapolis for shipment to boot camp. The awaiting Navy buses hauled us to the Greyhound station. Round trip bus tickets were issued to us, and I found that the bus schedule would work just fine for me to ride from Indianapolis directly into Akron, saving

Dad the need to come all the way to Peru to pick me up. I was in! I was a sailor! Was I ever excited as I boarded the bus and headed northward out of Indianapolis.

The trip back to our small farm near Akron was very exhilarating, but my heart was also carrying a sharp pang of nostalgia. I knew the stay at home would be short. The big strange world I had discovered in Indianapolis would soon become my world in which I had to survive. The young farm boy that had lived under the shadow of his mother's simple advise, would soon find that the big complicated world that existed outside of the Shewman farm and the little town of Akron was directly in front of him.

**The crossroads of America, downtown Akron, Indiana. The Eat Rite Cafe is the middle building with the Akron Cafe sign. Whether in or outside, this became the main discussion spot for war, women, and what's for dinner.**

I spent the next several days not engaged in any work for hire. Instead, I helped Dad do a few things around the farm. I recounted over and over to Dad and Mom the weird world that I had discovered in Indianapolis. They also thought it to be mighty strange. My friend, Byron, and I spent considerable time listening to his radio and projecting our thoughts into what the next few weeks might challenge me with. Neither of us had any idea what was around the corner for me. Many of the songs of the day used their lyrics to speak of the war and the encouragement of one's patriotism. I believe this helped pump me with anticipation and got me past the stress of worrying about the thought of becoming homesick.

During the few days of waiting to hear from the Navy, some of my close friends met with me at the Eat Rite Cafe in downtown Akron. I stuffed myself with all of the hamburgers and chocolate pie that I could possibly hold. I did not know just how long I would be gone. In my last couple years of school I had discovered what a hamburger was. I had always liked chocolate pie and learned how to devour chocolate pudding by the serving bowl. My mom and sister made sure I had plenty of chocolate pudding. I didn't think I would find any chocolate pie or pudding in the Navy.

Several of my friends and classmates had already left for service. As we one by one left the community, those that remained tried to show their interest in the one leaving.    In a small community such as Akron, each person is important.    When a person left our community, this usually communicated  to the remaining a feeling of sadness.    A small community in those days took on the feeling of being a family.    A caring thought that demonstrated real friendship was always deposited with those left behind.  I had noticed this to be true as others ahead of me left for service.  Wartime and the possibility of a family  member or local friend not returning alive was a reality.    The friends that I was about to leave behind gave me the opportunity to store in my hall of memories pleasant thoughts, as I prepared to depart for boot camp.  Many of my last hours in the Akron community were spent downtown in the Eat Rite Cafe cementing  friendships that would last a life-time.

When the day came to catch the bus to Indianapolis, Dad and Mom  decided that I should catch the bus in Peru, and then they  would have the opportunity to visit with my mother's sister who lived there.   Mom and Dad took me to the Peru bus station.  I hugged Mom and Dad one last time and boarded the Greyhound bus.

As the bus pulled out of the small Peru station  and started its journey to Indianapolis, I waved  one last time to my parents and watched them disappear from my view.   A huge lump welled up within my heart.  I for sure did not know how to anticipate what was ahead. The couple days of Navy life I had experienced in Indianapolis had started my thoughts to wandering. I knew it was going to be strange and a lot different from my Indiana farm life. The next few days and weeks would prove to change my life forever.

**Great Lakes Naval Training Station Main Gate**

25

**Administration Building**
**Great Lakes Naval Training Station**

# 2

# GREAT LAKES

## - the Start of Boot Camp

On August 17, 1944, at four o'clock in the afternoon, the representatives of the U.S. Naval Reserve loaded me and several hundred other new recruits onto an awaiting train in Indianapolis. I started, what seemed like to me, a long trip to the Great Lakes Naval Training Station, just north of Chicago, Illinois.

The train ride was exciting, for it was my second time to be on a train. Somewhere in Chicago's large train yard, I, along with four other homesick-looking new recruits, were loaded into a bright yellow painted taxi cab. What a weird color for a car, I thought. I had never seen anything like this before. I had heard of taxi cabs but had never seen one close up, let alone ride in one.

27

This cabby drove like a maniac.  Another vehicle stopped in front of us and seemed to be lingering too long to suit our cabby.  He got out and gave  the other driver a tongue lashing, such that I had never heard of or dreamed possible to utter.  They bantered back and forth in what must have been some hidden parts of the English language. At least I had never heard these sounds before. Finally, the debaters solved their differences just short of a fistfight, and my driver jumped back into his  cab.  He hopped the cab over the curb and  drove for about  fifty yards down the the wide cement sidewalk.  He hopped the cab off the sidewalk back onto the street and drove a short distance to another train station, considerably smaller than the Union Station.

It was at this point that I noticed there were many cabs just like the one I was in.  All were full of young looking men, hardly more than large boys.  I just knew that each was starting to feel somewhat homesick, and the thoughts of home were beginning to filter into their thinking.  For each of us, we were about to take on new manly responsibilities and chores.  For some of us, we would have to become better acquainted with our razor.

The uniformed Navy men in charge seemed to have ways of knowing who were recruits and began collecting us into groups. We were herded aboard another train that left shortly on tracks that followed the Lake Michigan shoreline. The train ride did not take long. It was dark and we could not see the lake, but we were told that it was there. The train stopped. I gazed out of the dark train windows and saw what appeared to be a very lonely place. Within two minutes we were ordered to leave the train. They did this by yelling out to us, "Fall out and fall in."

It seemed to me that while I was at Great Lakes there was always some little second-class seaman ready to shout this favorite naval command. Through our sleepy, one o'clock in the morning eyes, we managed to look bewildered, but yet expectant as we filed off of the train car.

It didn't seem to matter how late at night or early in the morning it was when the bossy second-class seaman demanded that we line up in perfect order for him to inspect. All of this was happening right there beside the train tracks. You might have thought he could have waited until later in the morning to get started. No, the Navy had its own way on how they wanted to greet us, even though we had just executed the greatest deed possible for our country. We had enlisted to fight for and defend until death, if necessary, our country.

We were herded around in a fashion that I thought was little different from the way I used to do the cows and hogs on the Shewman farm. Finally, the man in charge decided that we were in as good of order as we were going to get at this time of morning and started barking out more weird commands.    I found out later that all of these strange words that came out of his mouth meant we should get a move on.    I sure wanted to do things right, and  I made up my mind to do the very best I could.  I wanted no more trouble than I had to have.

We did just that and started our trek across the train tracks and across a highway  much larger than old state road 114 back home. We walked through  the largest gate that I had ever seen or ever thought about walking through.   We had entered The United States of America Great Lakes Naval Training Station.

I quickly let my mind zip back through all of the days and weeks of thinking about this occasion.  I asked myself if this was exciting?  I found that even at two o'clock in the morning, there was excitement.  What next?

# A Fart Sack, a Pillow and
# Two Wool Blankets

We continued to march deeper into the base in our column of twos.    We were now hearing a more shrill cadence call, the terms of which I could not understand.

Some old boy from Georgia had taken a training station assignment, right out of "boots," and was having the time of his life confusing some of us poor little farm boys with his non-understandable utterances. I was beginning to think that I was in some foreign country. Nobody sounded like him around my home town.

With considerable effort on our new leader's part, we found ourselves lined up about two-thirty in the morning outside the window of some all-night store they called a quartermaster's loft. We had been advised before leaving home what to bring and not to bring with us. The Navy did not want any more civilian duffel to ship home than was necessary.

As we walked past the open window of opportunity, some ol' salt tossed into my sleepy arms a thin cotton pad, about two inches thick and maybe thirty inches wide and a little longer than I was tall. He bellowed out, "Take this ol' fart sack, swabbie, this is going to become a part of your new home." I quickly figured out this new possession of mine that reeked with some peculiar medicinal smell was going to be my place of nightly rest. Part of this item description expression was a familiar term, but never in all of my sheltered life had I ever heard of one's resting place at night referred to in such a fashion. This action was quickly followed by a tossing of a small pillow and a couple Navy blankets that were cautiously caught in my weary arms. The all wool blankets reeked heavy of the strange smell that some of the city boys declared was a moth ball odor. I wondered if the odor would ever leave. I sure hoped so.

The line kept moving and we found ourselves in front of the building, falling into small groups of men they called platoons. As each of us stumbled out in the early morning hours, we had another exposure to the not so plain talking man from the deep South. By this time, I was so weary that I could have conked out on the ground beneath me.

Not too far from the place we were issued the sleeping gear, the Navy maintained several recruit receiving barracks. We quickly marched to the area and went inside of one of the buildings and were told to choose a bunk. We were also advised not to be too concerned about its location in the social atmosphere of things, because its use would only be for a couple of nights. I sure hoped the guys around me did not snore.

The next piece of Naval information I was given was the most unbelievable of all. The time was about three o'clock in the morning. The interesting fellow from below the Mason-Dixon informed us with much glee in his voice that we would be called upon at 4:30 a.m. to rise and shine. Just an hour and a half? I might as well not go to sleep. But with the moth ball odor, the thoughts of home and my bed   back on the farm soothing my thinking, I somehow drifted off to sleep.   I sure was beat!

## Day Number Two - a New Beginning

It seemed like I had just hit the bunk, and here they were, turning on the bright lights and yelling to us to "Rise and shine, you swabbies."   I jumped to the floor (later informed that it was to be called a deck) and examined my weary self.  I smelled of moth balls, since we had slept on a bare mattress and pillow.  We had not been issued any mattress or pillow slip covers. "Out front in five minutes," was the command from my new friend from Georgia or thereabouts.   "Fall out and fall in," was shouted to all of us in the barracks at the end of the short five minute segment of time.  This would soon became the command that we would hear over and over.

Prior to this command I had stumbled to the head (toilet), used the equipment and prepared myself   to stand out front in the unknown.   Out to the  front of the building I ran  as quick as my tired legs would allow me. I jumped into a part of the two rows of recruits we were told to form. I was finding that the Navy thought they had plenty of time and sometimes   they would just let us stand there and wait.

"Line up and dress right dress," I understood the sailor in charge to finally say. I knew that I had dressed right when I had left my home in Indiana. After all, I had not taken a thing off for the ninety minute snooze we had just taken. I guess I was too tired to take anything off or just did not know what to do. At any rate, here we were looking at one another, afraid to say anything, but each looking in bewilderment to the other as to what the dress right business meant.

"Okay, you bunch of goof-offs, keep your right arm straight down your right side, place your left hand fingertips so that they just touch the man on your left's shoulder. Turn your ugly face only your mother could love to your right and make sure your entire line of men is perfectly straight." All of this came belching violently forth from this little guy from some place that I knew had to be way south of Indiana. How could all of this come rolling out of one person with what only seemed like one breath of air, I quickly but very quietly pondered.

When it appeared to our fearless leader that we were dressed right enough to suit him, he yelled, "Attention!" Now we had to learn what he wanted us to do on this new command. I knew what the word attention meant, but I was not for sure just how he wanted me to stand. He let us know that with our heels together, our shoes had to be pointing one a little to the left and the other one a little to the right. All of this before five o'clock in the morning and with none of us not yet having any breakfast!  I wondered if my mom  was up back on the farm.  Maybe not yet, but if she were, I bet she was fixing a nice breakfast for Dad.  "Right face, ho!"  our man in command yelled.

I wondered just how long it would be before I would again put my feet under my mom's kitchen table.  The Indiana farm seemed a long way from where I was that early morning.

Trying to obey the command given, most all of us turned to the right, stumbling over one another as we made the turn.  "After chow, I will see to it that this never happens again," Mr. Georgia loudly informed us.  I sure wished he would talk like what I was used to hearing. With my not being used to "his southern accent," I was very fast becoming more and more homesick.  Dad telling me to get up and help do the milking would sound so nice about now.

We forward marched to the chow hall and there formed our first chow line of many to come.  We were paraded past stacks of stainless steel trays that we grabbed instinctively along with a knife and fork from tubs of what looked like had  thousands in them and moved on down the line like we were ol' salts.

35

## SHROUT - AFTER the MUD

Several Naval personnel, who must have been fresh graduates from boot camp, were behind the serving lines learning how to be Navy cooks. By the time I was in front of each of them, they had mastered the art of throwing what they called food into the sectioned off parts of my tray. No words were spoken, we just glared at each other. It was really too early in the day to carry on much conversation anyway. What was I to say? "Do you have your grain all thrashed or your corn laid by?" No, soon enough, they would find out that I was from the farm. I kept my mouth shut.

The chow hall was a huge place. Back on the farm, we probably would have predicted that the place would hold a lot of corn. Dozens of tables with built-in benches were all about. I found the first one that had an empty seat and dropped. I managed to sort through the scrambled eggs and find some that I thought were done enough for human consumption. They were so very runny. My mom had always fried my eggs sunny side up, and these were the first scrambled eggs for me in all of my life.

About every five minutes, some sailor would walk up and down the table rows warning us to be sure and eat it all. Man, I had to again sort through all of what had been pitched on my tray. I could tell that eating Navy food was not going to be easy. Oh well, perhaps I would get hungry enough that any of this half prepared stuff would start to taste good. I tucked the thought away in my mind and plunged ahead in the Navy eating process.

I managed to clean the tray pretty well. As I got up to find my way out of the chow hall, I noticed other recruits that looked like they had finished eating. They, for the most part, seemed to look like they knew what they were doing and were in another line waiting to do something. I joined their line with my tray in hand. We walked by a row of what appeared to be fifty-gallon shiny looking metal cans. We never had anything that looked like this on the farm. The man ahead of me was knocking his dirty tray against the insides of the can. I watched how he did it and followed suit. I tried to conceal on the tray, a few pieces of uncooked egg when I banged it in the can.

I learned later that the instruction on how to bang your tray was probably only issued once. Several months and quite possibly years ago, the procedure of what to do was probably given just one time and ever since there has been a continuous line in the Great Lakes chow halls. Each of us, as we made our first appearance at this chow hall, merely mimicked the man in front of us. The United States was at war and new recruits poured in by the thousands through this receiving center night and day. When I got back to the barracks, the discussion was going around that we all had been officially introduced to the Navy's official G.I. garbage can. We would learn later that they would have to stay nice and shiny and that we would spend a considerable amount of our time making sure this happened.

We had been instructed that just as soon as we had finished breakfast, we were to get back to the barracks and be ready for muster at six o'clock. By this time, they had us jumping around pretty good and we seemed to have plenty of time to get our food down, trays knocked in can, scrubbed with a brush and racked for the dishwasher. I even had time for a visit to the toilet (our fearless leader kept referring to this place as the "head"). What a name! I failed to see any eyes or ears that even caused it to resemble a head.

We reassembled in front of the barracks at the appointed time. Again, we went through all of this dressing right business. "You men will now start earning your keep," chided our fearless leader. "Right face, ho!" he exclaimed. "Forward, march!" Then all of the sounds that came out of the leader's mouth started running together and becoming not too clear to me: "Hip-hop, yo hite, yo hite, yo hite, hite, hite." These were all new words to me. Even on the most complicated days of instruction in Mr. Pontius' high school English class, I never heard him say there were such words in the English language.

We ended up marching right back to the chow hall. They assigned us in small groups to the several kitchens ("galleys," we were quickly told to say) that each chow hall seemed to have. I thought the place looked pretty good. The huge cooking ranges, of which my assigned galley had several, looked so much more massive than the Old South Bend cook stove mom used back home. I noted that the Navy kept them all looking very neat, clean and orderly. In a few short minutes I would have my evaluation of the cleanliness of the chow hall rudely and quickly changed.

The duty cook for that morning looked us over. We must have looked like a sorry lot. We were still in our civilian clothes, which by this time were really starting to look a mess. We were not given enough time to freshen up, a shave for those that had been shaving at home, or even do much of a job combing our hair. We all were in need of several hours of sleep. The cook must have been having a ball and laughing up a storm, though he did not let on. Did he ever look hard and mean! He simply scowled at us and pointed to some buckets containing steel wool and metal scrapers and gave one order, "Clean them up," he said, as he motioned to the cooking ranges. Again, I thought to myself, "This range I am standing in front of looks okay to me. What does he want?"

I started on the range with some steel wool in one hand and a scraper in the other.  I had seen steel wool while in my high school shop class.  We had used it to help sand  some of the wood projects we had worked on in class.  I scrubbed away with the steel wool like I was a real veteran and knew my stuff.  I found that if I used a little water with it I made better progress.  I started feeling small flecks of the steel  irritating my fingers, especially around the nails.

After I had spent about an hour on it, I  boldly inquired of the duty cook on one of his inspection tours, "How's this?  Looks good, huh?" I asked.  This was the first time that I had approached any of our assigned leaders with any kind of conversation. "Swabbie, when you address me you will say, 'sir!'", he fired back at me.  "And you are nowhere near finished in your cleaning assignment; keep going. Hell, it may take you until taps tonight," he bellowed!  I quickly found out that I was to address them all with, "sir." The second thing I learned was, he was not ready for me to quit cleaning the cooking range.

We did stop for a noon meal, and  about one o'clock I was back at it.  After being sworn at, of which I was not used to, I was beginning to believe that perhaps I would be at the task all night.  We were apparently cleaning in an area that had been secured for just this purpose.  No meals were cooked in this area.  Perhaps they rotated us back and forth from one galley to another. I hoped that this would be the only one I would have to be affiliated with.

The Navy wanted to see how quickly they could turn us around and for us to fall into their routines. Man, they won! If anyone would have said "jump," I would have said, "Where, sir, and how high?" I was quickly becoming a new boot even though I had reservations.

The bunk sure looked good along about seven that evening. I did not mind the smell of moth balls. They had a special welcome odor to this very tired young man. This welcome odor meant my best friend, the mattress, or fart sack as the Navy called them, was close at hand. I did not think I could have moved very far to find it. We had satisfied the duty cook with our bright and gleaming range tops. I had stumbled through the chow line again, lined with all of the ol' salt cook trainees. A quick trip to the head and I was ready for the sack. I remember the early thoughts before crashing, about what was happening back home and just what had I gotten myself into. But quickly, sleep took over my worn out frame. We were told that reveille would be at four o'clock. Oh, happy day!

## Boots, Day Three

Sure enough, four o'clock came and it seemed like only five minutes had elapsed in dreamland. The Navy did not awaken one in a gentle way. To a farm boy of the Great Depression days with no electricity on the farm, I thought the brightest spotlight possible was placed on my bunk. Some new, unfriendly, booming voice told us to hit the deck. Wow! I really came to. Sure didn't sound anything like Mom calling up the stairway back home to go help with the milking. Back into the same old civilian clothes we went, only by now, I could easily tell that I had been in the kitchen many hours the day before.

I sure would be glad to get uniforms issued. They had been promised for today. After the usual dressing of ourselves the right way, out in front of the barracks, we marched to chow. I was beginning to get the hang of how to act in the chow hall. It's funny what a couple of days in this place had done for me. After chow, I went back to the barracks to await the next order.

"Okay swabbies, fall out and fall in," came the command. Out to the front of the barracks we went a skittering. We quickly formed the required Navy line up

42

and set off marching to the sound of a new voice. The new voice was not much of an improvement as far as understanding what was being said. I did hear "your" once in a while and the word "right." I guess I was learning. Or, maybe the Navy had on purpose gradually brought before us leadership that was better educated.

At any rate, off we marched and sure enough, we ended up at the supply loft. The time to look like a real sailor had arrived. I was plenty excited about this part of the process.

The building we entered had a huge room with what looked like the world's largest checkerboard marked off on the floor. There were squares about three feet in size painted all over this large room with numbers painted on each square. We were told to stand on a number. Next we were told to get naked. The way the Navy said it was a little different. By this time, whenever I heard a gruff voice squall out at me, I paid attention. I started peeling off my filthy duds as fast as I could.

Each square was supplied with a shipping container. "Put every piece of your old stinking civvies in the box," the sailor man up front yelled. "We do not want to have to touch any of your damn smelly stuff. Hang onto your wallet and watch. You will get a ditty bag very shortly to stow them in," again bellowed the sailor in charge. Then we

43

were told to fill in the correct address of where we wanted the civilian clothes to go. An address label was on the box. This I did. I wondered what my mom would think when she opened up the box and saw the soiled clothes that she had last seen her youngest wearing when she said good-bye to him.

"Listen up, you dumb heads; I have some very important instructions for you," came the announcement from the front of the room. " I want the very first row to follow the arrow painted on the floor in front of you and stop where you see the word stop painted on the floor," "You will be told what to do when you stop," the man's very unfriendly voice said.

We did just that, following the arrow like a bunch of mice walking through a maize. When I got to the stop sign, I saw an open window, similar to the one I used to purchase orange pop through at Rock Lake, back home in Indiana. The man behind the window, tossed me a little white bag, about the size of one of Mom's flour sacks, and yelled to me, "Put this ditty bag on your left shoulder, take your peter in your right hand and follow the arrow." Man, nobody had ever talked to me this way before! I felt like some little kid that had gotten caught putting his hand in the cookie jar.

## SHROUT - AFTER the MUD

The next Naval experience that I was about to be introduced to would stay with me for the rest of my life. Ahead of me, in a darkened area, sat what I learned later was a Navy corpsman. He was perched on a short-legged stool, similar to what I would sit on to milk the cows back on the Shewman farm. This well-trained expert had a flashlight in one hand and was leaning over and looking at the guys in the line in front of me. He seemed to be paying particular attention to the area near their crotch. When I got up to being opposite of him, I found out what he wanted. "Okay Swabbie," he said, "you are next." In what seemed like just one breath, the corpsman said, "take that ugly looking thing you have in your right hand, skin it back and milk it down, don't diddle with it now boy, you can do that tonight." I stood in a state of shock as he shined the flashlight in my most private area. He glanced briefly and quickly yelled, "next", to the one behind me. I later was told that this had been my first introduction to a Navy "short arm" inspection.

As I stumbled ahead, my mind trying to absorb this new experience, I saw yet another corpsman, also equipped with a flashlight sitting on a small stool. The boot ahead of me had just made his appearance in front of the corpsman. I took my position about three feet away and heard, "Okay swabbie, face the other way, now bend over and spread your cheeks," the man on the stool commanded. The boot was quick to obey and was flabbergasted to hear the corpsman say, "Man, you have got shit up there!" The boot, not having adjusted to being careful of quick responses replied, "What in hell did you expect to find, ice cream?" This remark must have caught the corpsman off guard. I heard him chuckle and he quickly told the boot to move on.

As I took my position in front of him, I was really not sure what to expect. I was pleasantly relieved to not to have the man with the flashlight tell me anything. Apparently, I was absent of what my new friend in front of me had and I knew I was not hiding any dairy products. We were about to be issued a full uniform and all of the extra pieces that go with it. The Navy wanted us to possess a clean body and to be free of any social contact diseases.

As I progressed down the arrow marked route, I noticed that the man in front of me and the one in back were experiencing the same kind of bewilderment that I was in with all the new commands and routines we were going through.

Around the corner I came into a larger area. It contained some tables, minus anything to sit on. Our line passed by several windows that were located on one side of the room. The windows were like the blanket window of a couple days earlier. Each window had behind it a different part of the uniform that we were to be issued. We were asked to tell them our size and they in turn quickly tossed us the particular garment that they were in charge of.

My arms were piled very high when I left the last window of opportunity. I saw what the tables were for. We were given a stencil made out with our first two initials and our last name. On the table was a stencil brush and instructions on where to place our name on each item. Everything had to be marked with our name, even the shoes.

Every ten minutes or so, an instructor would stand up front and demonstrate how to roll up a certain piece of our assigned gear. He also demonstrated what items of clothing we were to put on to cover our nakedness. Strangely enough, all of the naked men around me were starting to look normal to me in their natural attire. Some more of the security I was so attached to on my Indiana farm was departing and I was starting to fit into Navy life.

The clothing included a pair of drawers (really boxer shorts), a skivvey shirt ( tee-shirt to some), a white undress jumper and matching white trousers. We were instructed to put on the undress whites. I looked around me and found that I wasn't the only one not knowing what to do. All of the other recruits were having the same

47

trouble as I in trying to stuff the pant legs into the "boots" (leggings). We had seen pictures and knew they had to be worn on our lower leg just above the shoe. The shoes we were issued and instructed to put on were of the work type with about a six inch upper and were shiny black. We learned later that they had to stay shiny black at all times.

We were quickly informed by the sailor in front of the room that once we were aboard ship we would have a limited amount of space to store our gear. "Therefore, we must all learn how to roll our clothing into small hard rolls," the instructor said. A sea bag had been issued to us at one of the windows we had stood in front of. The bag was about thirty inches long and when flared open, it would be about ten inches across. They informed us that between the ditty bag and the sea bag, we must be able to get into them all of our gear except the mattress, pillow and blankets. We even had to get our dress shoes into the sea bag. I found that the ditty bag was to be used for small personal gear, like shaving supplies, paper and postage stamps to write home. We had already been told to put our wallets and watches in the ditty bag and if we ever saw anyone messing with someone's bag, we were duty bound to report them.

When our group, which became my boot camp company, had rolled up all our gear and had it stowed in the two bags, we were ordered to assemble outside the supply area. Again we went through all of the dressing the correct way business in two long straight lines. Wouldn't you know it, we spoiled the nice formation lines we had made by falling out and   loading   onto Navy buses that were standing by. The buses took us out through the main gate that had made such a grand impression on me  only a few hours earlier.    Those last several hours were now seeming like an eternity.   But, I was determined to bear whatever the Navy would throw at me.  I had been yelled at, cussed at, and made to seem very stupid.  I could handle anything, I thought.

The bus trip saw us continuing down the highway in front of the Administration Gate, and in what seemed like a very short distance, turned in   through another large guarded entrance.   The bus I was on stopped as soon as the driver could after passing through the gate.   "Everyone out," yelled the sailor who had jumped into the front part of my bus.   He carried  a clipboard and  he sure looked official.  We lined up in our usual rows of twos.  The only thing different now, was that we were wearing a set of undress whites.   We must have been a sorry looking bunch.   I do not remember letting this fact bother me. After all, the leggings we now wore, gave credence to being called Boots.

We again   began to march, passing through row upon row of barrack buildings.  Each of the camps that we

49

had to go through was an eventful time. The inhabitants of some of the barracks we passed along the way really gave us a razzing. "You'll be sorry," and "watch out for that square needle in the left nut!" they yelled. Most of them were hanging from the windows they happened to be cleaning.

As we kept marching along, I was somewhat apprehensive about all of the advice and words of caution that I was hearing. My life on the farm bore fruits of experiencing feedback and advice from neighbors and friends that I could take as being fact. No one tried to steer me falsely. Did this mean that there was going to be some kind of object with four equal sides, and was it going to penetrate an area that I really knew was super sensitive? This did not sound good! I worried with that most of the night. I think many of the recruits also worried.

I had trouble the rest of that day dismissing the square needle from my thoughts. We had to march through several different camps before we reached Camp Porter. Camp Porter was the last camp in the line of camps. We learned that Camp Porter was to be our camp for boot training. Our company was given the number sixteen-ninety. We would keep this number for the duration of our stay in boot camp. I knew that I had arrived to what would be my home for the next eleven weeks. As we marched by row on row of barracks, I began to wonder to which barracks we would be assigned. I would find out soon enough.

Each camp had several two story barrack buildings. There were too many to make a visional count. Each barrack building had two entrances, and two companies would actually share the same building. The entrances were on opposite sides of the building. Our new home faced Fourth street and was on the corner of Ohio street. The front of our building provided a private assembling area. The other company that was sharing the building had their entrance on the back side and away from our view. Little did I know on that first day that I would soon learn every board in every step of that entrance.

## The Barracks, Home at Last

Bunk assignments had already been decided upon by someone prior to our arrival. We were greeted outside of the barracks by a third class yeoman. He called forty-eight names from the list on his clipboard. "You men whose names I just called, meet me on the upper deck," instructed the yeoman. "The rest of you proceed to the lower level and standby," he further ordered. My name had been called and I made my way to the upper level.

Our company, #1690, was comprised of ninety-eight men. The lower level had twenty-five sets of double bunks and my level, the upper one, had twenty-four to accommodate the forty-eight men assigned to our deck.    I noticed that we had been alphabetically grouped, as the first part of the alphabet  had been assigned to the lower level.

I had very little time to do any initial explorations of the upper deck.  Our new friend, the yeoman, went up and down the four rows of  bunks yelling out  our names and slapping a bunk as he read them aloud.   I was assigned an upper bunk on the very end of a row and close to the windows.   I thought that I had fared pretty well on my assignment.  My bunk buddy who was to sleep below me was named Slevin  and was from Tennessee.

We did not use first names and from the very beginning learned to use last names only.  I suppose one reason was the likelihood of several with the same first name. It would make it very difficult in giving a command, more than one might respond.   I never did ask why, and the Navy never bothered to explain why. They just did it this way.

I had no more than dropped my sea bag beside my bunk, when in came a second-class petty officer, who with a beautiful southern drawl, informed us that he was to be called Mr. Riley.   Mr. Riley was to be our Company

Commander. He tried to be curt and therefore "Navy like," but I could tell that he was going to have some difficulty in doing so. He was just too much a Southern gentleman to be in charge of a barracks full of "boots." But guess what, the Navy knew that. They saw fit to assign an assistant to him who was rougher talking and rougher looking than a wagon load of corn cobs. We found out that this assistant, who we were in quick order told to address as Mr. Pruitt, was only a seaman-second class who was not long out of boot camp himself. Wow! Could he ever cuss and swear! The way the fowl words came out of his mouth put fear in most of us. After all, we were not too long away from our parents and their tender loving care. Mr. Riley, in comparison to Mr. Pruitt, sounded and acted like my Sunday School teacher back in Indiana at the Akron Church of God.

Mr. Riley demonstrated what we were to do with our gear. Through the center of the lower and the upper decks, ran a large metal pipe or "jackstay," as the Navy called it. It was about forty inches off of the deck, just the right distance from the floor (deck) to hang our sea bag. We soon found out that we were to tie off the sea bag and ditty bag to the jackstay by using only square knots.

At this point in our Naval careers, no one, except for some of us that had been Boy Scouts, had any knot tying experience. I knew a few knots and I knew what a square knot was. The square knot was to become one of the more important knots that we would be dealing with during our stay at Great Lakes Naval Training Station.

Mr. Riley got us through this hurdle. He said, "Men, be sure you tie the square knot properly or you will be gigged for not doing so." He then demonstrated how we were to make up our bunk. "The mattress (he was so nice talking that he failed to use the four lettered word that we first heard it called) cover must be perfectly white and appear to be smooth, and tight to the mattress," he told us. He informed us that evenly spaced from each side and from the head to the foot, we were to have two mattress cover creases. "Men," he said, "Make sure each crease is at least one-half inch high or you will be in big trouble."

Wow! What was I to do? This all seemed very difficult to me. I had never paid much attention as to how my bed sheets looked at home. My mom took care of all the sheet washing and changed them when she thought they needed changing. I knew they did not contain one-half inch tall creases. I could see homesickness all over the faces of my barracks mates. I did the best that I could for the time we had at that particular moment.

It seems we only got started when we were yelled at by Mr. Pruitt, to "Fall out and fall in, and you had better damn well do it and on the double," he exclaimed! How

was I ever to make it through boot camp, I pondered? The
Navy had so many rules and regulations that really meant
nothing to this young teenager straight off the Indiana
farm.    On top of this, they had put this mean, foul-
mouthed  guy (that only a mother could love) in charge of
our company  to shout ugly words at us.  Would I survive,
I again pondered?

## The "Flying Five"

After we finished stowing our gear and making our
bunks, we assembled in front of the barracks and went
through all of the dress right dressing stuff.  Mr. Riley took
his place at the head of our column of twos and we started
marching to his commands.    His voice, in giving the
cadence commands, was so much more soothing than that
of Mr. Pruitts'.  There was absolutely no comparison.

**SP(A) 2/C  W. Riley (Mr. Riley)**
**Our company commander of Company #1690**

Down through all of the other camps we marched, ending up in front of the Division Headquarters building. We formed a single line in front of one of the doors to the building and slowly proceeded inside. In about twenty minutes, I found myself in front of a desk with a small sign indicating that the Navy man behind the desk was the paymaster. Already, were we to be paid? The paymaster said, "Shout out your name, rank and serial number." "Sign this chit!" he exclaimed! I had no idea what a chit was. I obliged him by signing my name on the small piece of paper that was pushed in front of me and did it as fast as I could. I was quickly handed four dollars and thirty five cents from the pre-arranged neat little stacks of money on the table. The chit then became a receipt.

As I moved ahead in the line, I saw up ahead of me what looked like about ten barber chairs. As I approached the area, I could see that each recruit only spent about a minute and a half in the chair. Each barber had a pair of electric clippers as his one and only tool! As I watched those ahead of me losing their long curly locks of hair, I realized that the barber that got me in his chair was planning to shave me bald. I soon learned what the sheep must have felt like when they were sheared back on the farm. I had experienced what the Navy called receiving our " flying five." I had been paid the first five dollars in my Naval career and had sixty-five cents deducted for the privilege of having a bald looking head.

## SHROUT - AFTER the MUD

The very first thing that I noticed after leaving the Division Headquarters building was the recruit marching in front of me and the peculiar looking bald head sticking out from his now too large of a white sailor cap.  He had the largest ears I had ever seen.  The peeled head caused his ears to stand out.  It appeared to me  the rim of his cap was riding in the groove between the ear and the bald head.  Did I look as strange?  I guess so.  I did not see a mirror in the shearing area and had no way of knowing what I looked like.  I even thought I could feel the wind blowing more.

My memory will always see the huge mounds of cut hair that was left on the floor of the Navy barber shop.  Some of the recruits had made a very large contribution to the pile of hair.  Red hair, black, brown and blond, all mixed together made an interesting hue to think about as we marched our way back to our barracks.  The Navy figured that if anyone had lice, the removal of all head hair would allow the scalp to be scrubbed more easily and perhaps get rid of the pesky critters.  I had been thrust into very close living conditions with many new guys whose personal hygiene habits of which I had no knowledge.  I certainly appreciated the Navy's objectivity in my behalf.

## Pin Cushion and Parade Rest Time

The third morning at Camp Porter found us in a long line at the drill hall. As we advanced through the drill hall in double lines, we were told to strip to the waist. We moved along the drill hall floor slowly carrying our jumper and skivie shirt in one hand, not knowing for sure just what to expect. I must have been in a line of several hundred men. Several other companies were there to experience the same unknown event. Scuttlebutt (Navy gossip) had it that we were to get vaccination shots.

I could see a coke machine at one end of the drill hall. Man, was I ever ready for a coke. I had developed a taste for drinking them when I worked at General Tire and Rubber. I was quickly and forcibly informed that I was in quarantine for two weeks, and the coke machine was going to be off limits for us sailor boys. I looked longingly at the shiny red drink box as the long double line proceeded down through the large quonset shaped drill hall. Two weeks was going to be a very long time, but I would just have to stand it, come whatever.

**Camp Porter Drill Hall still in use in the year 2000**

At a certain point in the drill hall, we formed a single line. As we moved along, we found ourselves moving up a slight incline that turned out to be dozens of bath towels stacked about fifteen deep. I saw a line of what appeared to be corpsmen on each side of the ridge of towels. The corpsmen were turned facing us. I just knew that each one of them was going to do something different to me. As I moved forward in the line I became more and more concerned just what that something was going to be.

As soon as I had made two steps onto the towels I was swiped on the upper part of each arm with a cold six inch paint brush loaded with alcohol. As I moved forward in the single file column of traffic, I tried to look from right to left to see what was happening. Somewhere out of space I felt multiple stings in both arms. I was being zapped by corpsmen standing on each side zinging me with needles. Both arms were telling me, ouch! It all seemed to happen simultaneously. "Move, mate," came the order from each of the corpsmen after he had done his thing. I did and whamo! It all happened again. A double hit with more needles. I could see blood ooze from the outer edge of my shoes as they mashed down on the stack of towels on which I was walking.

Thousands of boots had passed in this line earlier this day. Some poor boots had made quite a sacrifice. Some of the needles did not enter the arms properly and blood would squirt out and fall down to the mats made of towels. As the day wore on, the corpsmen just added more towels to the growing pile. The stench of alcohol, human blood and sweat assailed our nostrils with much vigor. Before I left the mound of towels, Snyder, who was the boot in front of me, fainted and had to be carried away. I had a sinking feeling myself, but I told myself to keep going. Snyder was given some kind of medical assistance and soon  rejoined our group before we left the building. There was not  much gold-bricking allowed in the Navy. If we were told to do something  we were to do it, or we would not have been told to do it in the first place. What genuine logic.

As we gathered after the evening chow in the barracks, we had plenty to talk about. Many arms were starting to swell and become painful. It seemed that those who had moved their arm  while the shot was administered,  or in some way caused extra punctures to be made, were complaining the most. My arms were a little sore, but I did not have any extreme pain. I had tried very hard to stand still and take it. I guess it paid off.

From the very first evening at Camp Porter, we found it necessary to spend considerable time washing the clothes we had soiled during the day. We had been issued a hand scrub brush and two cakes of P&G (Proctor and Gamble) laundry soap. I had never had to consider the washing of clothes while growing up. My mom always made sure I had clean clothes to wear. I quickly identified with the scrub brush and soap, making good use of them. The wash room was next to the shower room. The wash room had two very long scrub tables standing back to back with a water faucet above each scrub station. There were enough scrub stations to accommodate about half of my upper barracks. The table tops were covered with aluminum and had ridges built into them to help hold the clothes from moving all about the table while we did the scrubbing.

After the first day of exercise on the field grinder, a large paved area, I knew I would be getting lots of grass and tar stains on my undress white uniforms. I also discovered the first evening while doing my laundry that grass and tar stains were almost impossible to get out. I had to scrub and scrub with the brush and good old P&G. We were told to lay on the ground in doing our exercise routines. We had no say in it. After the second day of worrying with removing all of the tar and grass stain, I caught myself carefully checking the grinder surface before I plopped down on it.

August daytimes at Great Lakes were plenty hot. Some spots on the grinder had gooey, runny black tar exposed. There was no point in making my life more miserable than it was with unnecessary scrubbing in the evenings. The evenings seemed to disappear fast enough with all the things we needed to get done before lights out at nine. I was ready to call it a day, short though it seemed to have been. I was plenty tired!

Across the hall from the washroom was a drying room. It had many lines strung up about head high. We had been issued a supply of string, cut up into pieces about twelve inches long. Metal tips were on each end of the string to keep it from unraveling. We were instructed to call them "clothes stops." We used the clothes stops to tie our wet clothing to the lines. Each knot had to be a square knot and with all of the loose ends tucked in just so.

We quickly found out that the inspection team each morning would check the drying room. If you left dry clothes in the drying room, you got a "gig" or "happy hour." If you did not use the square knot properly in tying the clothes, another happy hour was issued to your credit. The Navy used the expression of "happy hour" to measure an amount of time you would have to spend doing some nasty, unwanted task around the base. This could be anything from scrubbing garbage cans in the chow hall to running errands for the Battalion office. If the officer in charge could not come up with anything when you reported to him, he might have you run several laps around the camp grinder.

From day one, we were placed on a duty roster and were required to stand various "watch" assignments around the barracks and at Battalion and Division headquarters. Many of the watch stations were maintained around the clock. Sometimes I would let my mind wander and consider the probability of all of the many men that had been standing in the same spot I was standing in for years prior to my three hour watch.

Some of my watch assignments were to stand at the top of the ladder (stairs) that entered our second floor level of the barracks. I was required to stand at parade rest during my watch. Parade rest is a more relaxed position, standing with feet and legs apart and with hands clasped behind your back. I wore boots (leggings) when on watch duty and was required to wear a guard belt. There was one guard belt for each watch station and it was passed on to the one that relieved your watch. A "guard belt" is a belt made to use with a holster and pistol. I wore the belt around my waist minus the holster and pistol when I stood those three hour watches.

While standing watch we were not allowed to talk with any other person that might pass by. Many of the night watches that I stood I thought would never end. To stand in the same position without conversation made three hours seem like an eternity. I welcomed the opportunity of an occasional interruption by a passing officer. We were required to come to full attention in the officer's presence and shout out our full name, rank and serial number. This kind of activity helped tremendously in staying awake through the three hours of watch duty while all of your buddies were sleeping. I did not mind this kind of watch duty, in fact I rather enjoyed it.

The barracks watch not only prepared us for the many long watches we would have aboard ship but also provided an excellent means of maintaining a fire watch during the night for the sleeping recruits. One of the many instructions given to those going on watch duty was to awaken any recruit that we would hear snoring. Snoring was not permitted. On one occasion an officer came through our barracks late at night and caught a recruit snoring. The person on watch had not awakened him and the officer made sure that the snoring recruit received in his face, the full contents of the "butt bucket." The butt bucket, was a three gallon bucket three-fourths full of water, and contained all ditched smokes from the night before. The poor recruit had to get up, clean up the mess, and get ready for inspection the next morning. He probably did not sleep too good for a long time after that.

On a couple occasions I was assigned to be an orderly at the mess hall. This was the only guard duty in boot camp that the guard was allowed to sit down and perform all of the duties of that particular watch. We were allowed to sit in a chair just outside the office of the duty officer, in both cases a WAVE (female officer). When anyone that came in, no matter who, my instructions were to jump to attention and sound off my name, rank and serial number. We had to do this to everyone that came in or walked by the station. Boots were not allowed to roam around, and this meant that anyone we would see in this area was a boot graduate and we had to salute them all. I found it necessary to jump up and down and sound off many times.

I had entered boot camp straight off the farm and had no idea that wooden floors could be so beautiful. The floors in the house on the old Shewman farm in Indiana had rough, uneven, splintery boards. The floors of the barracks really shined. It took a few days for me to get used to the slick and smooth wood floors. Each evening we would do the "Great Lakes Shuffle." Large fifty gallon "GI cans" full of steel wool were brought out each evening after chow. Each recruit would place a hunk of steel wool under his shoe and proceed to glide around the floor. If someone had been careless and left a heel mark, a little more scrubbing was necessary. From the second night on we watched each other and policed the scuffing around. We knew the spots created had to come up that evening.

We slipped around very carefully in our stocking feet, once we had the floors looking the way we wanted them for the next morning's inspection. We wanted the floor to look its best. After a few nights of pushing a piece of steel wool around with our shoes, Powell, a boot from Kokomo, came up with an idea of how we could respond to our future grandchildren when asked by them, "Grandpa, what did you do during the great war?" Powell replied, "I will tell them, 'Oh, I did the Great Lakes Shuffle.'" I thought that made pretty good sense and that I might use that comment someday.

Inspection each morning became fairly routine. However, during the first couple of weeks it was difficult. The Navy never seemed to allow much time to do anything. Some command-happy recent recruit graduate would burst into the barracks at four each morning, turn on the lights, yell to the top of his lungs, "Drop your cocks and pick up your socks and hit the deck you sons-of-bitches." Back home on the farm in Indiana, I had been used to my mom gently calling up the stairs, "Billy, its time to get up and go to the barn. Remember, Dad is expecting you, please hurry," she would say. What a drastic change.

We would have five whole minutes to use the head, make our bunk, get dressed, leggings and all, and be out front in perfect formation. One of the recruits, Steinberg, from Ft.Wayne, made an interesting request of the instructor one morning. He said, "Can't you awaken us at three-thirty and let us kind of mosey out?" I thought I heard the instructor chuckle under his breath, but needless to say, the drill instructor did not go along with this proposal.

## Barracks Before Bedtime

Evening chow started to become more interesting by the end of the first week. It would seem all of us were starting to forget how our moms had cooked for us. By this time we all were digging in pretty good into the food that the chow hall offered. Of course, we were so tired and hungry from all of the marching and the many jumping jacks that we executed tirelessly out on the Camp Porter grinder. I, for one, had not forgotten the way that my mom put delicious meals, one after the other, on the kitchen table back on the Shewman farm in Northern Indiana. I would constantly find myself thinking about what it was going to be like to go on boot leave at the end of the training session.

We were allowed to return to the barracks at our own speed after evening chow. Lights would be out at nine o'clock. In the middle of the barracks were four tables. They resembled a picnic type table with built-in bench seats, only these tables had solid tops. Here we could take turns sitting and writing to our family and friends back home.  We were encouraged to write regularly to our parents or as the case might be if married, to our wives.  It always seemed like the  time from evening chow until I heard the bugler play lonely sounding taps over the area public address system went very quickly.

Many of the recruits in my barracks smoked.  The smokers would patiently  await the opportunity to light up.  They had this chance when Mr. Pruitt with his  loud mouth, put his head in the doorway of the barracks and announced, "The smoking lamp is lit."  This happened in the small interval of time between  the fall out command in front of the barracks after marching for hours  and the next command to fall back in again to go for noon chow.  Lighting up a cigarette prior to that announced time was a no-no.  We would come back to the barracks after noon chow and would have a few minutes to rest or have open smoking again.  The smoking lamp privilege pertained only to the middle of the barracks area where the tables were located.

Some of the guys would play cards.  Most of the games had money riding on the results.  It was a time for small talk, the spinning of nostalgic stories and memories of home.  It was in this environment that I learned of big city life.  I became acquainted  with how it was to live in a row house.  I learned of a style of life that I did not know existed anywhere, even in books.  I found it fascinating to hear one recruit tell of his life in Fort Wayne, Indiana. I had always considered Fort Wayne to be the "big city." Fort Wayne was only fifty miles from the Shewman farm where I grew up, and yet I never went there.

My home town of Akron, Indiana had but one main crossroad. That was it. Everything commenced or ended somewhere just around the one set of corners. The road that headed east out of downtown Akron led to the Shewman farm. I learned this to be a fact when I became old enough to venture into Akron. There did come that day when Mom gave her permission for me to walk to town by myself. This east-bound road formed the one set of corners of the downtown square. I was finding out that the world outside my hometown area had many roads and many sets of corners. I quickly determined that I had existed for seventeen years traversing what some might refer to as a small "cow path" in rural America.

I became acquainted with my new barracks buddies in fast fashion. We were in a new lifestyle together. If I did not like the drill instructor you could count on it that the recruit next to you didn't like him either. Some of the talk would center on the school life that most of us had just completed. I got a big kick out of the southern drawls of the recruits from the southern states. In my little world in Akron I was very limited in having a variety of lifestyles to deal with. Most of my friends were sons of farmers or

71

lived in the small town. The town folk who called Akron home usually had strong family ties to someone on the farm.

Switchblade knife fights and many other gory stories I would hear discussed around the barracks during our early evening talk time. These were all new lifestyles to me. They seemed a million miles from the country life I had just left. It was during this type of talk session that homesickness and the nostalgia of family memories crept into my thoughts. Maybe I should have waited for them to draft me. This kind of thought quickly left me because I knew why I was there. I was there to learn how to whip the Japanese and the Germans in whatever assignment the Navy saw fit to give to me. Times were serious. I had my duty to do to my country. More importantly, I wanted to do this for my country.

## Mail Call - Much Better Than Chow

I quickly learned that mail call was the most important thing that happened in a recruit's day. It was even more important than chow. We would gather around the tabled area of the barracks during the noon hour and wait patiently for our name to be called out by the mail room orderly. I spent every evening writing letters to family and friends I had left behind. Family and friends back home were encouraged to write to the servicemen they knew. The home front was constantly bombarded with signs on street corners, store buildings, and in the the limited media, to write the men and women in service. I received a lot of mail. Some days I might have ten letters. Most of my barracks buddies received like amounts. There were some who didn't, and I felt sorry for them. Mail from home was great.

It was easy for me to imagine my mom sitting at the kitchen table writing to me. Taking the short trip down the hill behind the house to the mail box would be next. I could just see her putting the letter in the box and three pennies in the Ball Brothers can lid that was positioned in the front part of the box. The rural mail carrier would affix a postage stamp. Home was very important to me and a letter from home was the next best thing to being there.

On a few occasions I received packages from home. If the package looked like it could be a box of cookies, count on sharing it. If it looked like cookies to you, then it looked like cookies to your buddies. I always liked to share my home-baked cookies with my buddies. It gave me a chance to boast about my mom's baking, and that would lead into my giving more detail of her great meals.

73

It seemed to help tremendously to be able to talk about home. I found myself generating ways I could get into that sort of conversation. Home had a special place in a serviceman's heart. Finding myself away from home for the first time, and the fact of soon facing action and its unknown outcome, undoubtedly caused me to realize that nothing could take the place of home or the things which home represented.

All servicemen had free "franking" privileges and could mail letters free. I took advantage of this privilege and sent many letters home and to my friends. I wanted to hear from my family and friends. When I had read the last new letter I received each day, I immediately started thinking about those tomorrow would bring. I remember the weekends seemed to never end. It was nice to not have to do any drilling or exercising, but when Monday arrived it meant more letters from home and friends. The stateside letters that we mailed were not censored. This allowed us to tell them back home just how we felt about things. In my mind mail call was the most important activity that happened in boot camp.

# The Floating Ten

The Navy had instructed me on what personal toiletries to bring with me to boot camp. On the fourth day of boot camp, we again marched to the larger division building. While in the now familiar line of recruits, I was issued a double-edge safety razor and blades along with some shaving cream. They also tossed in a new tooth brush and a tube of tooth paste. I had brought these items with me when I came to boot camp. But some recruits seem to have to be told over and over again to shave each day. Experience had taught the Navy to be sure you had a razor by making you buy one even if you had one. The petty officer at the end of the line handed me a pay chit to sign. He then gave me seven dollars and eighty five cents. I was informed that I had now received the Navy's "floating ten," our second time to be paid. I had received the grand total of fifteen dollars in Navy pay with just four days work.

From that time on we were daily challenged to use our razor whether we needed it or not. Each day I would run it back and forth across my face. I was so thankful that I had used it the morning when the officer doing the inspection stopped in front of me and asked, "Mister, did you use your razor this morning and did you put a blade in it?" I was not used to shaving each and every day. I really couldn't see much growth in my beard in a twenty-four hour period. Mr. Pruitt squalled at us the very first day to "Put a blade in your razor and at least go through the motions of dragging it across your face." Oh well, maybe shaving everyday would assist my beard growing abilities. Time would tell.

## Barracks Inspection

From the very first day we discovered that we were to have very rigid barracks inspections. The officers making the inspections knew that we were a new company and I believe they were a little easy on us the first day. Some of the recruits started getting happy hours issued because of little or no crease on their mattress covers. The creases were supposed to stand up very noticeably from the head to the foot on the mattress cover. The cover was to be divided into thirds, thereby creating the need of making two creases. I decided that I would fold my spare mattress cover very precisely into thirds, and instead of rolling it up and putting in my sea bag, place it under my mattress at night and sleep on it. Each morning I took the one off I slept on and replaced it with the spare cover issued me. My body had never touched that cover and it was the one that I had slept beautiful creases into the night before; it really looked sharp. The pillow case had to be treated the same way. Others caught onto what I was doing and we started having good inspections on our barracks floor. Whenever I knew I would have need for a sharp looking jumper with the collar folds all pressed nicely, I used the same method.

I was standing barracks watch one morning during inspection time. I watched out of the corner of my eye as the inspection officer walked up and down the rows of bunks and swiped his white gloved hand up and under the bunks in search of dust. There were a few times that dust was discovered. Happy hours were assigned to the two recruits in the bunks where dust was found. I had heard about this and was thankful that my bunkmate, Slevin, and I kept our bunk dusted very carefully.

The lines that secured our ditty bag and sea bag to the jack-stay had to be tied with a perfect square knot and the loose ends of the lines placed in a perfect alignment to the knot and tucked into the top folds of the bag. The inspector was very fussy about how we did it.

As the inspection party moved about the barracks, they seemed to be looking for any speck of dust or the smallest heel mark on the deck (floor) to put on our report. We heard from Mr. Pruitt just as soon as the inspection party was out of earshot. "You God damn bunch of slobs sure screwed up again," he would scream out at us. "When are you ever going to learn to check the deck carefully?" he would bellow out in his deep, gruff sounding voice. "They found a heel mark about a quarter of an inch long by one of the tables. Damn it, get down on your hands and knees and check every inch of the deck," he squalled at us. Everything had sure looked good to me.

That evening we would spend much more time than usual going over each little corner of the barracks. Attention to detail became an integral part of us the longer we were in boot camp. This was part of the Navy's way of shaping us from a bunch of raw recruits into a close-knit group that did their thinking as a unit and not individually. It worked. We became very good at it. Soon we were winning the honor of carrying the regimental "rooster" flags as good ol' Company 1690 marched about the base. The flags designated several different areas of proficiency that my company started to get the hang of. That was what the Navy really wanted us to do.

## Barracks Life

Living away from home for the first time was a difficult transition for most of us recruits. Life in the barracks involved spending much of the intimate part of

78

living in very close quarters with total strangers. The other recruits around me seemed so strange. In the beginning, I did not feel comfortable being there and sharing the same space. I wondered how long it would take for me to get used to the strange talking and acting of the other boys that had joined up to fight for the same reasons I had. For the most part, the conversations that the evening time generated were very foreign to me. In a few short days, I noticed that I was starting to feel somewhat at home with this strange lot of young men that Uncle Sam had attracted into his Navy.

The Navy found a way of getting just enough scuttlebutt (gossip) into the stream of daily barracks life to keep us on our toes. We would hear about this and that of how we would be gigged for permitting certain things to become a part of our barracks life. We soon heard that it was correct to take matters into our own hands if we discovered that one of us was not bathing properly. There was such a shipmate. A boot by the name of Jonesy from South Bend, Indiana, seemed to not want to practice showering each day. It did not take us many days to discover this. After all, we were living in very close quarters.

One evening about ten of us in Jonesy's area grabbed him and carried him kicking and yelling to the shower room. Someone picked up a long-handled floor scrub brush and a cake of P.G. soap on the way to the shower room. Off came his uniform and skivies and down on the cement shower deck his naked body was placed and a scrubbing he did get. We tried to be gentle with the rough scrub brush, but even then many scratches and red marks appeared on his body. This treatment, rough though it may have been, found quick results in that Jonesy was usually first in the shower each morning after this incident. He never complained to anyone, including any of our officers. Scuttlebutt was that the Navy wanted us to use this method of alerting a careless boot to shape up and stay clean.

I thought the day would never end with all of the drilling and exercise time we spent on the grinder field. Most of our day's activities would end by four o'clock. We would spend about an hour in the barracks until the five o'clock chow time. After chow we would have barracks time until nine o'clock. Any free time we gladly retreated to the barracks. No where in my wildest imagination would I have ever thought the very first time I entered the barracks that I would soon learn to think of them as another home.

Home in Indiana was beginning to become just a memory and the barracks was quickly becoming my new place of retreat. Those early evening hours became precious. We were not yelled at in the barracks during the evening hours and we could feel a little bit of ownership to the few square feet around our bunk. There was no other place to go. This type of living would get us used to what it was going to be like when we went aboard our ship.

As the days went by, it became easier to share our former lives with one another. A lot of small talk was created in questions of "What did your old man do for a living?" or "Do you have a sister and do you suppose it would be okay for me to write to her?" Each evening went fast: there was laundry to do, letters to write home, and of course, we always had to spend a lot of time doing the "Great Lakes Shuffle".

Taps would be sounded over the loud speakers situated around Camp Porter. I can still hear the lonely sound of the bugler. Even with about fifty men on my barracks floor, I could feel the silence creep into the large room as if a feat of magic had occurred. With the snapping of the light switch, I now felt as if I were very much alone. The bugler always waited a few minutes after the lights were out before he performed his evening ritual.

As the bugler's sounds faded away across Camp Porter, my thoughts instantly would go back to my home in Indiana. I could almost smell the wonderful, pungent aroma of alfalfa hay curing as it lay on the ground. I certainly could imagine the sound of my mom's voice calling me to supper invade my bunk area as I lay there listening to the last sounds of the lonely bugler.

I'm sure the other recruits in my barracks were having the same thoughts and experiences. The sounds of the night that I would listen to from the upstairs bedroom back on the farm were not to be heard. There were too many human beings in training at Great Lakes Naval Training Station to hear anything else. We were all stuffed into a very small living area. All around the outside of the barracks, pavement could be found and not very much grass. The bugs and insects that make the night sounds did not want to be an inhabitant of this concrete world. I listened hard, but I heard nothing that I was used to hearing at night. Life on the farm had been fascinating with all of the sounds of God's little critters, as they busied themselves communicating in the darkness of those hot Indiana summer nights.

Meanwhile, back in the barracks, the activities of the day would soon remind my body that I really was tired. The thoughts of my mom's kitchen and the wonderful times I had spent around the table of that now very important room soon drifted away. All too soon, I would again be rudely awakened. It would be four in the morning and time to start the same routines of the day before. This was the way that the Navy did it: over and over until perfection could be reached. They did not settle for anything short of each boot complying with every jot and tiddle of the routines that had been passed down for decades. The young men from the cities, and those of us from the farms of the heartland, were beginning to become more difficult to tell one from the other. The Navy measured its success in training this way.

I think that each of us who shared the same long days of routine punishment of sore feet, aching backs, and dish water hands from all of the clothes scrubbing were beginning to think about the days in the immediate future. Would we stay together and be assigned to the same ship? We started talking about it. When a group such as a newly formed Naval boot camp company is treated all day long exactly the same, something starts to happen. It takes on the form of a close-knit family. Every member is equal in status. There are no favorites.

We were starting to become a team. We were breaking down any social barriers that might have been in place when we first arrived at Camp Porter. As a farm boy without a great deal of experience of how city life differed, I started to feel comfortable with the boots from the larger cities. We each received the same rations, dressed alike and were even yelled at en masse. We were becoming buddies. The barriers that life sometimes puts up started to gradually fall. We were becoming sailors. The boy from the hay mow and cow teat pulling was falling right in line with the young man from the big city grocery or factory. Each of us was beginning to understand each other's roots.

# Great Lake Tears

The Navy never did tell us in advance just what we were going to do on any particular day. We just fell out in front of the barracks each morning to await some new adventure. Each of us had the same inner hope that maybe we would not go again to the much dreaded Camp Porter grinder for more of those excruciating exercises. One such morning found us marching off in some unknown direction. "This is it," Powell was telling those in close rank with him in almost an inaudible low breath. "This is where we get the square needle," he warned us. " I heard it was to happen down this way. Henderson in Company 1688 told me so," Powell wailed. I believe every boot believed this thing about the square needle to be a real event. I could not think of just what this action would do to better my health situation. But again, I had never been in the Navy before and did not pretend to know all that might happen to me. Thousands of men before me had survived boot camp. I knew I would make it somehow.

After what seemed like a mile of marching, we found ourselves going down a narrow path and to the rear of some rather tall buildings. The buildings formed sort of an arena or open space. I noticed a small, one level building at one end of the open area. We were ushered into the smaller part of the building in groups of about twenty. Inside was a room that the twenty of us filled quickly. A second-class petty officer took charge and started to talk to us about gas warfare. So this was the real " it." We had heard all kinds of rumors about this part of our training. "Men, this might be the most important training that you will get at Great Lakes," the petty officer said. "Your life could very well be in the balance if the enemy chose to drop some poison gas on your base or ship," he told us. "Listen up, watch every detail about donning the gas mask you are now to pick up from the table in the middle of this room," he instructed us.

We all moved to the table and looked with much dismay at the weird looking bags stacked neatly upon it. "You will find a canvas bag on the table. Open the bag and remove the gas mask," the petty officer loudly explained. After my small group had done this, the officer continued to tell us what to do. "Place the mask on your head like this and make sure it feels comfortable," the petty officer demonstrated as he gave us instructions. "You will not want to move it one hair after you are exposed to the gas. Clear the mask of any gas that might have entered while you were placing it on your head. You will do that in this fashion," he said.

# SHROUT - AFTER the MUD

The petty officer in charge again demonstrated the procedure. "Close the outlet valve with two fingers on your left hand, or press the valve against the chin, exhaling vigorously," he said. "Now, pinch the walls of the hose tubes, and inhale. The face piece should collapse against the face. You should be all clear of any gas that might have slipped in while you were putting the mask on," he told us. "All set?" he queried us. "Now take your mask off and put it back in your bag. Put the bag over your left shoulder and follow me," he instructed. I found my heart jumping just a bit. I had no idea what to expect around some corner in front of me.

In a single column we followed the petty officer through a low narrow doorway into a darkened room. I really could not see much, hardly the man in front of me. " Halt," came the command, "check for gas," we heard the now familiar voice tell us in the dark. I was afraid to breathe. I just held my breath fully expecting to have some unknown giant knock me to the deck. "No gas yet swabbies, but there will be. Continue to follow me," he told us. All of a sudden, someone detected a strange smell. I couldn't see who it was but it sounded like Powell who was in my group. Then I smelled it. It was a burning sensation to my throat and nose. No orders were given. We were in a real situation and must act on our own. I took my mask out as quickly as I could as I held my breath. I put the mask on, blew out the bad air and found myself afraid to test it. I mustered up some courage and followed all of the prior issued instructions and tested the mask and found that it really worked and that I could actually breathe.

"Forward march," came the command. We lurched forward through the dark, trying to see through the mask. Whamo! My head banged into a wall. We had been led into a low ceiling corridor and some of the recruits lost their masks in the confusion. Those that dropped their masks were yelling and screaming and gasping for air. My mask managed to stay put and I kept moving forward. All of a sudden, welcome rays of daylight burst forth. A large doorway appeared and I could feel the fresh air rushing in. The maskless recruits rushed outside, coughing and gasping and stumbling over one another. What a sight! We had been given a small dose of tear gas. I came through this exciting adventure unscathed. I felt like a real veteran.

After a few minutes of some of my buddies hacking, coughing and wiping tears, we were ordered into formation by Mr. Riley and told to stand by at parade rest. The last of our company emerged from the gas chamber with all of the same reactions, and in short fashion we all formed up and headed back to the barracks. When we got there we were given a short break so that the smokers could smoke. Then back we went to the grinder for more exercise and drill. Dad used to tell us back on the farm that when there was nothing else to do, we could always pull weeds. I guess the Navy had similar ideas; no idle time for any of us.

# The Rigging Loft

The following day found our company marching its way toward what we heard later was the rigging loft. All kinds of ropes were tied in all kinds of funny looking shapes and knots. They were not holding up anything or keeping anything from wandering off. "You swabbies listen up," shouted what was probably just a boot graduate. "From this moment forward you are never to use the word that is spelled by these four letters: r - o - p - e. You are gazing upon many configurations and uses of knots that can be made from line. The U.S. Navy is proud of the word line. Your new word is line and don't you forget it. If you say the unforgivable word, around the grinder you will go fifty times without stopping," endlessly he continued. To a farm boy, we had a lot of uses for the forbidden word. I could tell that this was going to be a challenge. I wondered if this hotshot in charge had ever made hay. Putting up hay in the barn required a lot of use of ropes.

## SHROUT - AFTER the MUD

We were told to pair off with someone. We were starting to get better acquainted with some, more so than others. Most of our marching formations found us lined up alphabetically. Slevin was always right in front of me so we paired up. Besides, we were bunk mates and beginning to get well acquainted through our joint housekeeping efforts. Each of the pairs faced off across the jackstay that was secured about waist high. There were enough stations for everyone in the entire company to get a location. I was about to see if my early days in Boy Scouts would be of help to me.

We started with the basic square knot which we had already learned to master from tying our ditty bags and sea bags to the barracks jackstay. There were enough different knots and objects to build from lines that we found ourselves coming back the next day for more instruction. I enjoyed working with lines. While in the Boy Scouts back in Indiana, I learned several basic knots, and found this most helpful. The Navy had in mind that we were to learn all of their basic knots, such as: the bowline, the running bowline, sheep shank, half hitch and the double half hitch.

We were given some instruction on the various methods of splicing lines. Splicing is a method of joining the ends of two lines or of bending a line back on itself to form a permanent loop. We were told that the the loops on lines made mooring of ship to dock much easier. Those assisting on shore had to but throw the loop over a chock and the ship would be secure. If properly put together, a splice was as strong as the line itself.

We learned how to make "monkey fists" and "fenders." Monkey fists were small balls fashioned on the end of a line called a "heaving line." We beat and pounded the small ball, about the size of a tennis ball, until it became very hard. The open end of the heaving line was attached to the "hawser," a much larger line used in mooring a ship in port. The heaving line is carefully coiled; about two-thirds of the coil being held loosely in the left hand (if you are right handed) and the rest of the line with the monkey fist on the end in your right or heaving hand. We practiced by heaving the line to a make believe shore for someone to catch, and then they would pull the large line to the pier they were pretending to be standing upon. The monkey fist shaped like a ball made it easy to get the line to the spot you wanted to tie up to. We had to practice this heaving act several times. I found out later that I would use this process over and over when I was aboard ship.

A "fender" is also made from line. The laying out of fenders is necessary prior to going along side another ship or pier. The fenders vary in size. Common are those of about six inches in diameter and thirty inches long. After spending two full days in the rigging loft, I began to feel like a real sailor.


# Picture Time

As we worked our way through the first month of boots, I began to think about what I would look like in uniform. I just knew that I was beginning to look like a "real salt." After all, up to this point I had not received any gigs or happy hours. I thought I looked pretty good when I looked in the head mirror. My way of wearing the uniform must be okay. Sure enough, after we had been at Great Lakes for about a month, we found ourselves marching to a spot at one end of the grinder where there was a four row bleacher. The bleacher was just the right size to hold all of our company. There were so many companies coming through the training center the bleacher and photographer were busy most of the time.

A company picture was made and singles of each boot were taken. Three boots from my company were from Fulton County, Indiana, just as I was. Miller was from the town of Fulton, Denton and Nichols of Rochester, and of course myself. All three of my Fulton County barracks buddies had been rivals. Every year through high school we met on the athletic battlefield. It was in softball or

91

basketball and usually several times each year. Now, we were learning how to pool our energy and efforts in our Country's "ultimate competition." We had a Fulton County picture taken. We received the pictures we ordered in a few days and I immediately sent one home.

**Ol' Fulton County Sports Rivals**
**Left to right - standing - Miller and Nichols**
**Kneeling - Shrout and Denton**

**Author, Bill Shrout, looking quite confident**

As I let my mind wander back over fifty years ago, I can see the tree we stood under.  There was a piece of rock, probably part of some huge boulder, sticking up from the ground.  For our single picture shots, we were instructed to stand on the rock.  During the time of the writing of this book, when I visited Great Lakes, I was privileged to stand on this same drill field.  The tree had long since vanished but I thought I saw the rock.  My mind raced back to that bright September morning in 1944, when all of my barracks buddies, one by one, took their place, standing in this memorable spot.  We were on that day memorializing our adventure into the ranks of the United States military.  I just knew that this would be a day in my life that I never would forget.

## Maggie's Drawers

The next day after the picture taking experience, we did our usual falling out and falling in.  Mr. Riley was starting to become somewhat proud of his Company 1690.  I could see it in his eyes as he checked our ranks for correct formation.  We could now line up quickly and with each boot taking great care to not be off so much as a hair.  Does one suppose we were really becoming real sailors?

"Men, today we will have the opportunity to show our marksmanship on the rifle range," Mr. Riley happily told us. "Let's look our best as we march from Camp Porter through all the other camps to the range. A lot of new recruits will be watching us, and we will want to look sharp," he told us. We all liked Mr. Riley. I think we would have tried anything he asked us to do. We quickly fell in step behind Mr. Riley's soft utterance of the now familiar cadence call. What fun it was to feel fresh and with much vigor in our hearts, as we paraded through the other camps! I was starting to feel strong, healthy, and glad to be in the U.S. Navy, doing my part in defending our country.

We arrived someplace still on the base, but yet quite some distance from Camp Porter. It had taken us about 40 minutes at regular marching speed. There was a long row of five foot fencing with an opening ever so often. I could see what looked like benches located ten feet on the far side of the fence. A few feet more and the view was lost to a down hill grade. It indeed was the rifle range. I told myself that this was going to be a lot of fun. I loved to shoot a rifle!

We were told that we would be shooting 200 hundred yards at targets on slight downhill trajectory. I had never fired a high caliber rifle before. A twenty-gauge shotgun gave a big enough kick to cause me to give it lots of respect. Firing the .22 caliber rifle on the farm at rats and sparrows was going to be a far cry from the kick this big looking gun was about to render to my shoulder and perhaps chin! We had spent some time in examining this rifle in preparation for this eventful day. I knew how the basic piece was dismantled and put back together. I knew to always give it my finest respect.

This was it. We had to look like we were anxious and real sailors ready to shoot and hit the bullseye. I really felt a lot of excitement in the air. I quickly remembered the reports that filtered back to my Indiana farm from those from our community who had gone into service ahead of me. They would write back telling of winning marksmanship medals from their shooting expertise. I was just stepping up the size of weapon that I would use. I told myself I could handle it.

I counted off with the rest of the company and found myself in a group of eight, assigned to a particular shooting station: one of the benches that I had observed as we had approached the range. A Springfield model 1903A was in inventory at each bench. The rifle is of the bolt action type, and its magazine had a capacity of five rounds. Man, was it ever heavy. I wondered just how I would manage to hold it up to my cheek for any extended periods of time. I soon found out the answer. Each boot in our company had the same thoughts and apprehensions running through his mind. We all were fresh out of an environment that did not have heavy-duty firearms as standard equipment in our homes.

A non-booted sailor seemed to be in charge at each shooting station. I learned that he was a recent boot camp graduate that had been given a few hours extra training about the rifle and assigned to the rifle range. He quickly divided us into two teams. My group was told to proceed to the walk path at the extreme port (left) side of the range and to go to the area immediately behind our target. I could barely see the target. It looked so far away. Surely we would not be expected to hit this small looking spot every time. I'm sure we could hit and miss and make it once in a while.

We scampered off as directed and soon found ourselves in the "butt" area of the rifle range. What a weird name to give the area. We were given instructions how to check the target after each firing and how to patch any holes those firings might make.

My target patch team quickly inspected the target for holes and since nobody had fired yet, found them to be ready for use. We stood by for the next instructions. "Up targets," said our "butt area" commander over a loud speaker that only we could hear. With this command, we pulled on a small line (rope) and hoisted the target about five feet up in the air in the special track. With this action, the guys back at the firing bench  could see what they would be shooting.  I held my breath.  I had no idea what to expect.  Over the large loud speaker system, that not only addressed the firing area but  our area as well, came the command,"Ready in the butts."   Then came a pause. "Ready on the firing line," was the next command,  Was I ever ready!   My entire body was alert and alive with anticipation.   Then came the two unforgettable words of that day, " Commence firing!"

At that point I thought a war had broken out.  Even as far removed as we were from the position of the men and rifles, it was extremely loud.  One would have thought the high bank of dirt we were hiding behind would have absorbed more of the sound than it did. Later I was to find out that it was even louder when it became our turn to fire the rifles.

The firing lasted for only about fifteen seconds.  We then grabbed the small line hooked to the target frame and hauled the target down to our eye level.  Three of us were assigned to each target to make the patch repairs.  My buddies and  I quickly noticed that our shooter had made only one hole.  He had hit the outside edge of the target. Not good but at least he hit the target once the first time. The firing sessions were repeated over and over for about a dozen tries by each shooter.  We noticed that as each volley was fired, the shooter became more and more accurate.

After about an hour of this "butt work" we were told to return to the edge of the area and retrace our tracks back to the shooting area. It was a little spooky even to do this. I kept imagining someone being careless and discharging their piece in my direction. It didn't happen. I returned as fast as I could to the firing box that I had been assigned. I was the first to pick up our assigned rifle. Man, was it ever heavy! I was ready. I knew that this was not going to be too tough. After all, I had experience shooting rabbits with the "ol twenty gauge" back on the Shewman farm.

I did a couple shoulder wraps with the rifle sling and dropped to a prone position on the ground. The seaman (boot graduate) in charge handed me a clip of live ammo. I inserted the clip just like I had done many times with mock clips in earlier dry run drills. I started to take aim on the target that now looked like it was on the other side of the world. Man, it was small! After much bobbing around with the barrel going first this way and then another, I started to get over my nervousness.

"Ready on the firing line," came the voice ever so close this time. It seemed like he was really talking to just little old me. I held it where I thought the trajectory was

99

about right. "Commence firing," the man in charge yelled! I squeezed the trigger ever so lightly, the rifle roared and I thought it jumped a full foot. I waited for the "butt men" to do their job and to report back to me. What I saw was a red something or other being waved in the butts. "Oh, you got a 'Maggie's drawers,'" the man in charge of my area said. Getting a red flag waved at me meant that I had missed the entire target and had received my notice by the waving of Maggie's drawers. Enough of this I thought. I could do better than that. I did much better the next attempt and before my shooting session was finished, I had hit three bulls-eyes, as well as several shots placed close in.

I felt much better on the return march to the barracks. After chow time had come and gone and I had finished my daily washing of clothes that had become soiled, I decided it would be big stuff to write home about the rifle range experiences. I did and I knew my mom was now starting to believe her little Billy was perhaps really growing up.

## Pulling Boats

Two days after the rifle range experience, we marched to an open area that had, what looked to me, to be a couple of oversized row boats. The only boats that I was familiar with were small, about 12 feet in length, flat-bottomed fishing boats that Roy Landis used to rent to fishermen who wanted to fish Rock Lake. These boats were much larger. They had five wide bench seats, plus a smaller seat in the stern. I learned later, a person they called the coxswain, would sit there. He would hold a small funnel shaped contraption that looked like a smaller version of the megaphone used by the cheer leaders at Akron High School. He would shout instructions to those of us that had hold of an oar.

Our mission this day was to become familiar with the boat commands, positions of the crew and in general, a good overview of small boats, Navy style. We learned terms like: stand by the oars, up oars, shove off, out oars, give way together, in bows, stand by to toss, and boat oars. Other commands were: trail, hold water, stern all, back starboard or port, and point the oars. I didn't think I would be able to remember all of the different commands. I hoped that they would not test us on them. They didn't.

After we had spent about two hours with this instruction, we fell into our usual marching column of twos and headed back to the barracks. It would be the usual noontime chow hall routine, a few minutes of leisure time, and time awaiting the next command to "fall out and fall in."

After noon chow was put away, out front again we went to once more complete our now most familiar routine of company formation. " Men, we now will put to practice what we learned this morning. We will go to the boat basin. It is a long march, so lets be on our way," he informed us in his usual calm style. I was beginning to like Mr. Riley.

The boat basin was located on Lake Michigan. It took us nearly an hour to get there. Several boats similar to the one we drilled in earlier that morning at Camp Porter were at the waters edge awaiting us. We broke up into small groups and were assigned to a boat. I remember sitting on the port (left) side which seemed awkward to me for some reason. We had a boot camp graduate act as coxswain of our boat. He thought he was hot stuff. We went through all of the commands we had learned earlier, only this time we actually ventured out onto the lake a short way. It seemed interesting enough, but I wondered if there ever would be a time that I would actually use this drill in real experience. It seemed to me that the Navy thought this to be a part of the old routines that had been passed down for decades and were not going to stop just because there was a war on. It beat the drill routines that we never seemed to get enough of back on the good old Camp Porter grinder.

# Manual of Arms

The Navy decided it was about time for us to learn how to use the rifle in a different way. We were to start doing our exercises using the rifle as an object to toss around. We marched to a new place for our morning activity and were each issued a rifle that for all practical purposes seemed very real. But they were not. We started the first instructions on how to handle the piece. They informed us that "piece" was the correct name for what we were holding and that we were not to say the word gun. I decided I would pay attention to that command and stay out of trouble.

We learned: order arms, trail arms, port arms, present arms, parade rest, and how to open the rifle and hold it for inspection at the command of an officer. "Some day soon," Mr. Riley told us, "We can count on this happening."

I thought we would never stop using the arms for physical drill. This was hard work and took a lot out of a young buck like me. All of the instructions of down, forward, up, and shoulders seemed to never end. Then we had to learn how to make the diagonal and forward lunges. There were "sweeps" and "twists" to round out the rigorous exercise routine. I always was glad to see the time for the practice rifles to be put away. Even standing in line in the chow hall was starting to look good to me. Uncle Sam, and the merciless men he had in charge of my well being at the Great Lakes Naval Training Station, were starting to change the habits and thinking of the farm boy from Indiana.

## Big Butt Betty and the Other Girls

During our eighth week we were introduced to aircraft identification. We marched in columns of one through a large building - no windows or lights and through one narrow corridor after another. As we progressed to our destination I noticed that it became darker and darker until you could not see your hand in front of you. We stumbled around and found chairs to sit on and to await the next order. Our entire company was intact in the same room. We waited for what seemed like a very long time. But we were all content, to the very last man, to just sit and not to be doing jumping jacks or some other exhausting kind of exercise.

As we continued to wait for the next instruction, I noticed that my eyes were starting to become adapted to the black surroundings. "Men, you are now becoming night adapted," the officer in charge told us. "The purpose of this exercise is to get you familiar with not only our friendly ships and planes but also with our enemy," he remarked. "We will be flashing silhouettes on the screen. Slowly we will decrease the time you will have to view each object. You will be able to recognize them in as little as 1/100th of a second before we finish this part of your training," he informed us.

If one has never tried to identify something in a fraction of a second, let me say that it is very difficult. We learned after three trips to the identification school how to be very alert and ready to yell out the name. Fighter planes were given American male names like Zeke, and bombers were given female names like Nell or Kate. The one with a large bomb bay area was tagged "Big Butt Betty." Whenever Betty was flashed we all got a charge out of shouting "Big Butt Betty!"

## The End is In Sight

More and more drill, day after day - we now were getting pretty good.  Some were even getting used to Mr. Pruitt.  We were learning how to not displease him and stay ahead of his thinking on what he was going to yell at us next.  I suppose this was good training for us.  Mr. Pruitt was certainly someone that was very difficult for me to understand.  Why did  he have to act like he did?  People back home were never like this.  My neighbors and school friends respected my abilities as I did theirs.  As I look back now, these had to be some of the most formidable days of my young adulthood.  I was finding out that there were some pretty crummy characters out there in the cruel hard world.  I had been sheltered in the small community environment in which I had grown up.  Now I was in the real world and would have to adjust and be ready to deal with any situation or character that might come my way.  I did not necessarily like my situation, but I was determined to survive.

Week twelve came and slowly passed to the beginning of what we now had been told would be our last week, number thirteen.  We were never told exactly when we would graduate.  I heard that the amphibious corps needed men and they hurried us up. We had a week's notice. Mr. Riley sounded as though he was going to miss us. Mr. Pruitt didn't seem to care much. I didn't think I was going to miss him too much, either.

Graduation day was a bright sunny day the 3rd of November. We took more care this day in getting ready. We all put some extra effort to our boot shining, our boot lacing, and the way our pant legs fit into them. To the drill field we went. It was such a pretty day that the exercises were held outside. On the inclement days the huge quonset type drill halls were used. There were three marching bands playing exciting march music. I was really pumped. All of the graduation ceremony exercises meant I would soon be going home on leave. I could almost smell and taste Mom's home cooking simmering in the kitchen.

We really strutted our stuff. How exciting it was to hear the Navy bands playing so loud and clear the stirring marches. One could almost forget just why he was there in training. War meant learning how to kill, and at the very least, destroy our enemy. As we went through all of our "eyes right" and hippity hop business, I felt a lump well up within my throat. "Little Billy" at last was a man and a full fledged sailor, at that. My, I felt tough, like I could whip a bear! I probably was in the best shape physically I had ever been. The Navy had put me through every conceivable exercise known to man. We all were ready for the next chapter in our new adventure; that of our new Navy life.

Company 1690 stepped pretty high on our way back to the barracks. After chow time at the now familiar chow hall, we were off to our last boot camp instruction school. We went into what one might call a theater. We sat down and had about twenty minutes of film on how to act when we left boots for our first leave. We were warned on what to expect from the local ladies while at the train stations and bus terminals. I was tutored on the latest in social contact diseases that were supposedly running rampant out on the home front. We were given instruction on what to use if we were to relent and participate in some of the activities that would be readily available to us.

The last evening in boot camp was spent laundering any clothes items that needed it. We all wanted to look nice when we arrived home for the first inspection by our individual families. We still did not know what our next assignment was. Scuttlebutt was that the amphibious corps wanted us. We were instructed to only take our sea bag and ditty bag with us on boot leave. The sleeping gear was lashed into our hammock and left in a special storage area located at Division Headquarters. We would pick it up when we returned from leave, only the Navy would have it transferred over to the main gate area. We were told to report back there by 5:00 p.m. on November 15.

I finally got to sleep. My mind kept racing to Dad and Mom's house on the farm just east of Akron. Sleep did come. At 4:00 a.m., Mr. Pruitt came in for the last time to awaken us. I thought I saw a smile on his face. I even think he was proud of our company. We were good and he knew it. Maybe, just maybe, I could learn to like him, also.

I splashed water on my face and went through the antics of shaving. My few whiskers had yet a long way from looking anything like my dad's heavy-duty growth. We practically ran all the way to the chow hall. We sure did not want to be late on the day of our first official leave.

After we had gone through another mustering procedure, we were given tickets to go to our various homes. All travel was done by train. My closest rail site was Plymouth, Indiana, and my round trip ticket cost all of two dollars and ninety-five cents!

With tickets stored in our ditty bags, and sea bags on our shoulders, we said goodbye to the barracks that we would never see again. This was a building that while living in, had changed our lives forever. In no way would we ever be the same. We had learned about new cultures and what it was like in the big cities. Some city boys now had a small glimpse of what life might be like down on the farm.

We assembled for the last time outside the barracks There were no wet towels to swat us as we walked out this time. What a wonderful feeling! As we stood in perfect formation of parade rest, Mr. Riley gave us his last bit of advice. He said, "Men, the safest way to live the Navy life is to always carry a paper doll. When you think you have to have that certain male physical need, you can tear off a piece and not have anything to worry about." What a nice guy! I shall never forget him. He was the perfect commanding officer for me to have for my first exposure to this new outside world.

## Red Caps Everywhere- Salute!

We marched the reverse of the very same route we first came into Camp Porter. We were on our way to the Main Gate area and the train tracks where thirteen weeks earlier this green recruit, straight off the farm, had first gazed upon. Quickly, Mr. Riley said his good byes, and we were dismissed to board the awaiting train to Union Station in Chicago.

I found my way to a seat on the yet not too familiar vehicle called a train coach. Talk about adrenalin flowing, man it sure was in me! I was going home and this was the first leg. When I entered the coach, a porter wearing a red cap approached. I came to a full salute. After all, he was wearing a billed cap and that is what we had been doing for the last thirteen weeks, paying respect to all billed cap wearers.

The train ride to Union Station was quick. Here I found myself cast among thousands of other sailors, all going home for the first time. I quickly learned one thing. I was not the raw recruit that first came through Chicago earlier. With all confidence I found the train schedule board and found my gate for departure to Plymouth.

The ride to Plymouth did not take long. Most of the time was spent getting out of Chicago's train yards. As soon as the train could pick up some speed we were soon slowing down for Plymouth. After the train finally came to a stop, I got off and asked a local red cap, without saluting him this time, which way to U.S. Route 30? He told me and sure enough I found it and was on my way. I intended to hitch-hike. I had been told that the civilians were very obliging to picking up service men. Sure enough a car stopped. What luck! It was Hugh Wildermuth from Akron. He drove the the thirty miles or so to Akron and would only have it that he take me to my parent's farm. Another nice guy! I was beginning to realize that indeed I had a lot of great friends back in my home town.

Ten days of freedom, WOW! After Hugh let me out of his car, I got down and kissed the ground. I really did. Home at last! This certainly had to be the best thing for this farm boy this side of heaven! All of the many times I had let my mind wander back to my mom's kitchen, while listening to the sound of the bugler's lonely taps as they drifted across Camp Porter, were at last coming to life.

The timing for my arrival home from boot camp was just perfect. Mom knew that I was coming and had a great meal on the way when I arrived about 5:00 o'clock that afternoon. I was home for the next ten days and I was going to enjoy it. I spent that evening and the next nine evenings and days catching up on telling my parents and friends all about Navy life. Never in my life did nine days go so fast and I soon found myself packing my sea bag and ditty bag to return to Great Lakes Naval Training Station.

I said good bye to Mom which was very difficult. This was a time in the calendar of WWII that did not allow one to expect to get to come home often. Most service men home on leave wondered if coming back home might not ever really happen again. Dad drove me in the '33 Ford back to the train station in Plymouth. He told me later that it was very difficult to see me go.

I was quickly becoming a veteran in living in the world, for I had always been so dependent on my parents in decision making. All of the where-to's and how-to's had been decided for me most of my life. Now I had to say yea and nay to the attendants of the games of life, whether it be red caps, cabbies, or those behind the store counters. For the first time, I was making purchasing decisions for the items being offered as the "breads of life."

**Inside view of the quonset shaped drill halls at
Great Lakes Naval Training Station**

# 3

# And NOW, ON WITH The WAR

## Back to Great Lakes

I had left the Akron area early in the day and I arrived at the Main Gate of Great Lakes Naval Training Station about noon. I was in no mood to eat and went straight to the area marked for returning boot camp graduates. One thing about the Navy, they sure liked to have you follow signs. They had plenty of them showing us just where to go.

Many of my new friends were already in the report back area. We exchanged the usual "what we did," and now it was time to get on with the next adventure. Late afternoon, a secondclass yeoman came into the middle of the barracks and posted some lists on the bulletin board. I hurried over to look. Sure enough, there I was, on a list that seemed to include everyone in our old company 1690. We were going to Ft. Pierce, Florida, to amphibious school

115

to become gunners. I had scored pretty high on the medical and electrical examinations, and had requested submarine duty. The submarine idea came from watching early war movies. I found that my wishes did not seem to be of any concern to the Navy. The advance rumors were correct--they needed men to man some of the Navy's landing craft and no one seemed to object. The other sailors were as much in the dark as I was. None of us knew for sure what was around the corner for us. We had enlisted to help win the war and most of all, keep from walking our fool heads off as an Army doggie.

I had no idea where Ft. Pierce, Florida, was located. I knew where Florida was from all of the maps I had drawn in school and the map races I won so easily as I came up through Akron Grade School. We learned that our bed gear was ready for us in the same barracks we had reported to. The Navy had seen to it to move it there while we were on boot leave. I claimed mine and repacked the sea bag in the middle as instructed. I was ready to go.

## Florida Bound

We heard the order to fall out in front of the barracks. I had thought that perhaps I would not have to fall into that old boot camp routine again, but not so. Here we were again. Oh well, I was in the Navy now. With gear on one shoulder and our ditty bags hanging from the other shoulder, off we went to the awaiting train coach. A lot of card games had been played while in boot camp during the leisure pre-sleep time period. Whenever we found ourselves non-occupied, cards it was. I had never played as much cards as some of the guys. I had never gambled and I learned quickly that is what the rest of the guys wanted to do. Not me, I refrained, for I didn't like the idea of possibly losing my money.

The train ride was exciting for all of us. Most of the guys had not spent much time on trains. I thought it was interesting listening to the car wheels clickity clacking over the railroad ties. I even became bold enough to go from car to car. We had to do this to get to the dining car. All in all, one could say the atmosphere of the men aboard was that of anticipation and being just plain curious.

Through the night and the next day, most of us were adding new names to our list of places we had been. Names that had been only referred to in our geography classes were now being added to our adventure list. We crossed several different state borders on our way to what was awaiting us in Florida.

Ft. Pierce seemed to be a sleepy, quiet town. The early November morning air had a warm feel to it, almost a soft feeling. Arriving in the middle of the night had its own unique way of cloaking the thinking of this country boy. I truly was seeing and hearing new sights and sounds. I told myself that this must be what it was like to travel to a foreign land.

We filed out of the train with our gear and were loaded onto waiting Navy buses. The bus left the train station and quickly crossed a short bridge span to what appeared to be an island. The United States Army had been there before the U.S. Navy and had gouged out a camp on what had been a forsaken, useless, sandy piece of land. According to what my boyhood training had taught me, I did not believe this land would grow much corn. It seemed to me the Navy was working very hard trying to get me to forget this early farm knowledge. All they wanted me to think about was ships, water, knots, guns, and war.

The bus stopped and we unloaded. We were assembled in small groups of sixteen. Somewhere in the dark a tall, lanky sailor from Kansas by the name of Goheen, told us he was in charge. I saw that he had second-class petty officer strips on his sleeve. With Goheen at our head, away we marched. The sand made it difficult to stay in step. It seemed to me that we would take two steps forward and then slide back one.

We walked perhaps a mile and found ourselves marching through rows of tents. We stopped in front of some tents and were divided into two groups, eight men to occupy each tent. My tent buddies turned out to be Shopoff from Ft. Wayne; Morgan from Illinois, and Morris from Michigan; and an older rough talking character from Southern Indiana. There was one huge guy from upstate New York by the name of Kloss. He looked like the strong man, Atlas, I remembered seeing in the newspaper ads. Little and Newberry, both from Georgia, made up the list of our tent family.

Not much conversation was made in our preparation to retire. It was two in the morning before we got our folding cots ready for sleeping. I had never slept on a folding cot before, but I was tired and it felt good. I had arrived in Florida and was ready for my next adventure. Sleep came fairly easy. Memories of my family and friends from back up north in Indiana faded from my thinking.

"Up and at it, fall in like two rows of Kansas corn," came the low but firm command from Goheen. He had been standing right outside our tent flaps. I jumped up and quickly put on my dungarees and shoes. Out in front I went, but quickly learned that Goheen was not going to be like Mr. Pruitt at boot camp. I knew right from the beginning that this guy was going to be a real buddy and shipmate.

119

**Tent City on the Naval Amphibious Training Base**
**Fort Pierce, Florida**

120

## SHROUT - AFTER the MUD

We did a little of the group formation stuff we did at boot camp, but quickly found ourselves marching, rather draggerdly, toward the chow hall. It was not too far away, and we came back on our own to the tent. This was the only time we would march as a group to chow. I suppose the Navy just wanted us to know how to get there. From then on we could either go or choose not to go during the certain chow hall hours that were posted.

Back at the tent, Goheen told us that for showers we were to go over towards the beach and use the open shower areas provided with salt water straight from the ocean. On my first trip over I discovered just how close we were to the Atlantic Ocean. We really were close. The salt water shower left you feeling sticky. The Navy wanted us to get used to what might be our lot in life on-board ship. We might have fresh water rationing and switch to salt water for showers. The next day, our leader Goheen told us go to the Post Exchange and get some salt water soap. It would actually lather up, and one felt like, just maybe, he was getting clean.

We were quickly informed that the main reason we were at Ft. Pierce was to learn all we could in as short a time as possible about firing 40 mm guns. Our exposure to the 40 mm at boot camp was very slight. We had one opportunity to stand up close to the single barrel gun and put one clip of ammo into it.

Here at Ft. Pierce we were introduced to the twin barrel 40 mm  The gunnery range seemed like it was about three miles from our tent.  We would trudge out there every few days.  Walking in the sand was really tricky as you really did slide back as you walked.  The second day in camp we were issued our sand shoes.  It was a light colored work type shoe with about a six-inch top.  The sole was designed to grip the sand better than our boot camp issue.  The sand shoe was very similar to the shoe we used in boot camp, only the boot camp issue was black and looked a little dressier.

I had  heard about sailors and their exploits on liberties that they always seemed to be on.  We did get several opportunities to go on liberty in Ft. Pierce.  We walked the length of Hutchinson Island, across a bridge that spanned the inlet and ended up almost in downtown Ft. Pierce.  Morris, Kloss, and I would walk over to Ft. Pierce and eat at one of their eateries.

One time I was with one of our buddies that had been nick-named "Dog Shit."  As we were returning to our tent area, D.S. began to feel his oats.  He had consumed a little too much of the  spirits that Ft. Pierce had offered him and it was starting to show.  As we passed by various tents, he would slam his fist into the boards that were on the lower couple feet of the tents.  Sometimes the boards would burst and splinters would fly, and I would hear someone yell out in shock. They never knew what was happening, because we kept right on moving, only to have him hit yet another tent with its wood siding.

This tent board-pounding buddy was from Indiana and would tell tales about the days of John Dillenger and of the fact he knew this famous gangster. He said he dated John's sister. This was far out for someone like me who had been absolutely nowhere. On one of the occasions when D.S. again had too much of the spirits offered in town, he really zonked out. I had to carry him by looping his arm around my neck and half dragging him. I convinced him that he would have to straighten up as we passed the guard at the gate. He managed to do this, at least enough to satisfy the guard on duty.

When I got him back to our tent and stretched him out on his bunk, he vomited into his bunk and lay in the vomit and blew bubbles as he breathed. My cot was next to his, making my head only about three feet from his. I had never experienced anything like this in all of my days on the farm.

I finally became tired of looking at the mess and listening to the sounds he made blowing bubbles. Besides that, the horrible smell it caused was really getting to me. I rolled him over on his side and propped him so he would not roll back down into the mess. I scooped and scraped up the mess  and tossed it into the GI can that was outside the tent.  It still stunk in the tent!   Oh well,  anything for a shipmate.

## Faith In Mae West

One morning we marched  to the far end of the island where the LCVP's were tied up.  The  LCVP was a small boat used to take  troops ashore in a beach landing. The Navy was using this end of the island for training other sailors how to man the small craft.  We were instructed to get into the small boats.  Our group did just that, filling up six boats.   They issued each of us a life jacket, dubbed "Mae West,"  and out to sea we went.  When we were out of sight of land we were told to jump into the sea.  We were informed that the tide would eventually take us ashore, but we could speed the process up if we would swim some.

I soon lost sight of any of the other guys.  As the large ocean swells tossed me up and down, I was beginning to feel pretty lonely.  I started paddling with my arms and kicking with my feet, but  I did not seem to be getting anywhere.  Each time I would rise up to the top of a swell I would stretch my neck as high as  I  could, hoping to see land.  After what seemed like an hour, I could start to see the shoreline. What a welcome sight to see land. When I finally floated up on the beach I found that I was only a short way down range from our tented living area. What a surprise. I had been in the water about two hours. I had started to look a little wrinkled from the long exposure in the cold salt water. The Navy wanted us to experience something of what it could be like if we lost our ship and had to go into the water. This large body of water, called the Atlantic, looked so very much bigger than the Rock Lake that I swam in back home!

I was starting to make some mental notes about the vastness of the mighty ocean, especially when I was alone in it. If it looked this big to me, when I was just a couple miles or so off the coast, then what was it indeed going to be like out in the middle of the Pacific? My home in Northern Indiana was starting to seem farther and farther away. Life and the big huge world I had heard my mom talk so much about was starting to seem a reality.

## Raking the Beaches

We had not been at Ft. Pierce very long, perhaps three days, when the Navy decided we needed some exercise in humility. Dozens of us were given regular garden type rakes and were told to form a line of rakes.

**The very beach the author raked while at**
**Naval Amphibious Training Base - Ft. Pierce, Florida**

Each man had to stay a couple feet behind the man to his left. This way we were able to make one continuous rake mark as we drug them across the open beach. I imagine this exercise had more than one value. True, it did make pretty marks in the sand. Still, it could flush out any foreign objects not desirable to a bare foot.

When we had made one complete set of marks going parallel to the beach, we did a ninety degree turn and made another set of marks crossing perfectly the ones we had just made. We would do this for what seemed like a couple of hours. Only those of us that were not petty officers were required to perform this "warlike" task. I have often wondered if the other men thought this to be a frivolous task like I thought it to be. It did not make much sense to this farm boy. I had never seen so many garden rakes before nor since, for that matter. Some garden tool manufacturer sure made a haul on this idea.

We had the second gunner's mate join our group. His name was Gallagher and had a heavy Southern drawl. We were to learn later that we were the complete above deck crew that would have, as their general quarters assignment, the loading and firing of anti-aircraft guns on our ship. The two gunner's mates were to be in charge of the guns and show the rest of us how to be good gun crewmen.

SHROUT - AFTER the MUD

Each morning after chow, the routine became to fall out into formation in front of our tents. Almost every time, Gunner's Mate Goheen, would tell us to fall in like two rows of Kansas corn. Most of us had never been to Kansas to see the corn grow, but this Hoosier farm boy sure knew what a couple rows of Indiana corn resembled. Off we would go slipping and sliding in the sand to the gun range. Somehow this was a lot more relaxed formation marching than when we were in boot camp. Each of us felt like we were seasoned sailors. We were about to become real "old salts." The anticipation of what was ahead for each of us gave new heights to our excitement.

We spent a lot of time standing around the twenty and forty millimeter guns. The gunner's mates would use what knowledge they had acquired at gunner's mate school. Some days we would actually shoot the guns at sleeves towed by small Naval aircraft. The plane would tow the sleeve, which was a bright colored cigar-shaped target about fifteen feet long, at the end of a long line behind the plane. The pilot would stay out over the Atlantic Ocean. We could then shoot out towards the sea and not endanger anyone.

I was starting to get used to the loud sounds that the forty millimeter made. We were given plugs to put in our ears. That helped to soften the concussion and made the noise tolerable. After about a dozen rounds had been fired I was ready to take a rest. The excitement of pushing large shells in clips of four into the magazine, and having the extremely loud sounds of the rounds exploding so close to my ears, was somewhat stressful and of course painful.

On the very first day at this gunnery range, when it came time to have noontime chow, we were introduced to a new and short way to take on nourishment. The Navy called it "C-rations." We walked through a chow line and were handed a small package that looked like the entire small box had been dipped in sealing wax. I remember something similar looking when I watched my mom preserve food products on the farm. The wax sealed the carton and kept it fresher, and I guess it also made it waterproof.

This proved to be the only place I would have to eat C-rations while in the Navy. I thought they tasted all right. There was not much quantity, and I still felt a little empty when I had finished consuming the entire packet. I had been issued a knife that had an opener that I used to open the couple small cans of meat. With the cookie type crackers that were in the package I could get by for the noon meal. I sure would not want to eat them for any great length of time.

# There Goes the Captain's Car- Salute!

The first morning after we arrived at Ft. Pierce we were given a very valuable piece of information. We were told about a large, long black car, probably a Chrysler or Lincoln. I never really did get to look at it when any thought of its recognition was in mind. I was too frightened to look for detail that would tell me what kind of vehicle it was. Goheen told us that there was only one automobile on the base, and it was assigned to the base Commander, Captain Gulbranson.

There were a lot of trucks but only one car. Whenever we were to see the car coming, no matter from what direction, we were to stop immediately, face the car, give a full hand salute, and hold until the car was out of sight. Goheen said, " Men, you may think there is no one in the car besides the driver, but don't you worry. Mrs. Gulbranson and her dog may be the only ones in the car. Salute anyway! The car may look empty. Salute it anyway. Hell, you may be just saluting the Captain's damn old dog. That's okay. The Captain gets madder than hell if he catches someone who does not salute his car whether he is in it or not."

This was our introduction to the base commander. I remember on several occasions finding myself walking along the base road coming or going to the Post Exchange or base laundry and starting my hand salute when the car was a couple blocks distant. The car also had the Captain's flag flying from a holder on one of the car's fenders. I did not know that there were any people like this in the world. There certainly were not any around Akron where I grew up. The idea that I would have to bow down and scrape the ground never set too well with me. I will always remember that particular time in my Navy career.

Most of the guys in my group used the services offered by the base laundry. If one has never tried to wash their clothes in salt water, they have an experience to behold. Salt water is bad enough to use for a shower; it makes your body sticky. Washing clothes in salt water can be done, but is not very desirable. The clothes never feel clean.

I found it to be fascinating to be able go to the base PX and purchase sandwiches and soft drinks. The prices were very reasonable, and I found this to be quite an interesting way to eat. I had never seen anything like this around my home. Besides that, I was growing tired of Navy style cooking I had experienced in boot camp. I found that I could down several milk shakes along with a few sandwiches. This bill of fare sure was a far cry from the food on Mom's table or the chow hall.

The weekends were free time to us. Most of us found it important to go into Ft. Pierce on liberty. However, it was also very relaxing to just lie on our cots and enjoy the gentle warmth of the weather that this part of Florida offered to us Yankee boys from up north. I would be scooting around in some of Indiana's early snows if I were home. I found it quite satisfying to write to Mom and Dad, and of course my brothers and sisters, and tell about that part of my good fortune.

I could tell that I was starting to be more resigned to my lot in life--that of the Navy. I still found myself thinking of home and what they must all be doing while I was down in Florida. My family had been a very close-knit family. We spent many Sundays together enjoying the tasty spreads of food that Mother would set on the table. We had just come through the Great Depression, but that had not deterred Mom in the slightest. She could whip up a feast from what appeared to be nothing. Lying on my cot, looking up at the top of the canvas tent, somehow brought these wonderful memories out in vivid detail.

Two summers ago, before this writing, my wife, Julie, and I returned to Ft. Pierce. As we drove across what is now a new bridge, my mind raced back to those

132

days of over fifty years ago.    Even the area around the bridge quickly brought back the memories of holding upright my intoxicated shipmate we so fondly had learned to dub, Dogshit. The resurgence of that past experience of safely guiding him over the old bridge and back to our tent and the awful mess he created,   flashed to mind. The tented areas were gone and in their place were plotted city streets all filled with modern homes. These homes  housed, in most cases, another generation of people.   The people that walked these streets probably never realized or had any inkling of what went on there more than a half a century ago.

As I rounded the curve and headed towards my old tented area, I passed by what was then the administration building that housed Captain Gulbranson and others on his staff.   It was still there and looked about the same as my memory said it would.    Some parts of it   had been remodeled and I fully expected that to be the case. After all, it had been over fifty years since I had last had the opportunity to see it.   When I was stationed at Ft. Pierce, I never had the  need or the courage to enter the building. Saluting the car that carried the man that was the principle occupant of the administration building was enough.  I did not want to have any unnecessary encounters with the Captain.

When I reached what I thought was about where my tent had stood, I saw a real estate office covering the approximate spot. We went inside and chatted a few minutes with the realtor on duty. I quickly informed her that her desk and office were now sitting about where my old tent was positioned during my stay in Ft. Pierce. She of course knew some of the history of the island, but I am sure she was not aware of such a personal revelation that had been revealed to her that day.

Julie and I left the real estate office and walked along the beach. I reminded her that this was the approximate spot where I had washed ashore, wearing my faithful "Mae West" on that unforgetful day long ago. I could almost feel the sensations of that day, as I imagined the wet and cold eighteen year old, whose skin had wrinkled from the exposure to the salt water, wobbling as he attempted to walk in this very same sand. I paused and gazed out to sea, hoping my recollections would ignite and allow me to once again, review the thoughts of what fueled my youthful mind that eventful day.

**Former Administration Building
NATB - Ft Pierce, Florida**

THIS MONUMENT DEDICATED, ON THE FIFTIETH ANNIVERSARY, JANUARY 26, 1993, TO THE MEN AND WOMEN OF ALL ARMED FORCES WHO SERVED AT THE U. S. NAVAL AMPHIBIOUS TRAINING BASE FORT PIERCE, DURING WORLD WAR II, FROM JANUARY 26, 1943 TO FEBRUARY 2, 1946.

**Author, Bill Shrout, leaning on a dedication monument**

# 4

# TRAIN TIME AGAIN

# - WHERE NEXT?

## All Aboard

Our Naval stay in Ft. Pierce was short. After all, it did not take a lot of time to show us how to operate the guns we would find on our ship that would soon be assigned to us. One of the last things we did was to spend some time on a small ship called a sub-chaser. The sub-chaser had one single barrel forty millimeter gun that provided some actual sea experience in loading and firing.

Six weeks after arriving at Ft. Pierce, the Navy decided we had completed enough training to move on. Just a few days before Christmas, we packed all of our gear into our sea bags and ditty bags and followed Goheen and Gallagher in a column of twos to downtown Ft. Pierce to the railroad station. Excitement was again in the air and the thought of going to our next assignment was invigorating! We boarded one of the Navy's troop train cars ready for us at the train station in Ft. Pierce. Scuttlebutt had it that we were to get more training on a ship similar to the one on which we would see action.

As we pulled out of the Ft. Pierce station, I was beginning to like some parts of Navy life. I rather enjoyed train travel. Even though the troop train car was a little crude by today's standards, I thought of each trip as a new experience. On the way out of town we passed by what proved to be orange processing factories. We made a short pause close to one and some of the workers tossed my buddies and me some oranges. This was a real treat for me. To have an orange to eat while growing up was a rare happening.

From time to time we traveled along the coast line dodging in and out from vantage viewing points of the surf. I remembered geography well enough to believe we were going north. I wondered what the next assignment would be. We traveled all night and soon the next day our curiosity was satisfied as we unloaded at the railroad station in Washington D.C. Into a bus I went, gear and all. I soon found myself stumbling around under the weight of the gear on the Navy base called Deer Creek. We were in Virginia, close to the Chesapeake Bay.

We were assigned to a barracks and found several new faces already there. By this time we were beginning to gather up what was to be our ship's crew. We were now adding the below deck sailors who went by the name of the "black gang." The enlisted men of the black gang wore a red ring around the left sleeve of their dress uniform. Those of us that carried an above deck assignment had a white circle on our right sleeves.

We arrived at Deer Creek on Thursday. No duty was given to us the rest of the week. I recall spending a lot of time in the PX, where I saw my first ball point ink pen made by Reynolds Company. The PX had it priced at seventeen dollars. I thought that was a small fortune, but I was so fascinated with how the pen worked that I bought it. As I remember, it did not last but about two weeks.

Monday found us on-board an LCI (landing craft infantry) and with a lot of unfamiliar faces. We had more of our crew assembling, some of whom were to be our new officers. Ensign Warren Anderson was our new gunnery officer. Now he really was supposed to know all about it. I was assigned to spend my time learning everything I could about the forty millimeter. I was to become a first loader. This meant that I was the one to push the clip of four rounds of ammo into the gun. I received the clips of ammo from the second loader who retrieved them from the racks positioned all around the inside wall of the gun tub.

As we left the sight of land that first Monday morning, we readied our guns for practice firing. We were getting used to watching the Navy pilots tow long skinny red sleeves attached to the end of a long line. A few times we were told the pilot had radioed down to watch out: we were missing the target and shells were exploding too close to his plane for comfort. Four of us--the pointer, the trainer, myself, and another first loader--rode the gun turret as it moved to follow the target. The gun was a twin forty and each barrel required a first loader. Just the slightest movement or adjustment on the part of the pointer or trainer could spell trouble for the pilot towing the sleeve. They controlled the side to side and up and down movement of the gun barrels by turning small wheel shaped cranks. Looking back, I realize this was a pretty risky assignment for the pilot.

I learned a new term while stationed at Deer Creek. It was called a "midnight requisition." The second time out on the LCI we spent a couple of nights on-board. We had need for some supplies and it was after hours on the first day. Someone knew that the building where the supplies were stored happened to be unlocked. A detail of men, that included myself, was dispatched to go get the supplies. We did and were advised to say nothing about the matter. It was explained to us that we would be taking the supplies under the authority of a "midnight requisition." It was late at night and it all seemed very appropriate to this farm boy. After all, there was a war on. That fact made a lot of things we did seem correct. I thought nothing about it since I was not in charge and was ordered to complete the assigned work detail.

Christmas was just around the corner. I sure would like to go home for the holidays. But Christmas Eve came and went with no leave. Two days later we were informed that we would be given a six day pass. Wow! It sounded just fine to me. I very quickly packed a few things in my ditty bag, lined up at the office doorway, received my pass and boarded the Navy bus that would take us into the train terminal at Washington D.C. What an exciting time! I could just about smell the cooking aromas from my mom's kitchen.

The train trip across the Eastern United States was very enjoyable. I felt that I was a full fledged sailor and that I had earned this short leave. The scenery of snow ladened trees as we passed through the countryside was so refreshing. Here and there I could see farm buildings and some activity of the residents as they scurried about doing the chores with which I was very familiar. I wanted the next six days to last forever.

Sadly, the six days went fast. I spent several evenings with friends in Akron, swapping stories and wondering together about what was around the corner for all of us.  My brothers and sister came home on the Sunday I was there.  We had a wonderful family time together.

A huge snow storm invaded the home area the last day of my leave.  The last night home found me getting back to the house after midnight.  I managed to get Dad's old '33 Ford car stuck in a huge drift in front of the house.  Dad was easily awakened and with the help of our faithful horse, Charley, we managed to dislodge the car from the deep drifts.  The car had to be available for Dad to take me to catch a train in Warsaw the next day.

Early morning came and I remember well the final hug good-bye with my mom.  One never knows going off to war if or whenever they will see their loved ones again.  Times like these settle heavy in one's mind.

Dad and I drove the twenty miles or so to the Warsaw train station in silence.  Both of us were thinking about what was going to be happening to me.  Returning to the Navy undoubtedly meant that I would be going overseas.

Dad stood beside the tracks and watched  the train pick up speed as it  departed, carrying me and heading for Washington D.C.  Dad told me later that he felt as if the train was  pulling  him  onto  the  tracks.  Now  that  I am also a parent, I know that it must have been very difficult for parents to watch their sons and daughters leave for the service, not knowing what the future held.

As the train sped on through the cold heading for Washington D.C., I had plenty of time to reflect upon the good life that I had been privileged to enjoy. I thought of the hard work my parents had gladly expended in my behalf. I knew that I, along with the new crew of sailors we had formed, would soon be headed into harm's way.

No one could predict for sure what events history would record. I could only reflect on current news I had heard while home and on the fact that many of my local community's stalwart youth would not be returning from battle. As I watched the strange countryside flash past my rail car window, I wondered about my future.

Country living and the rewards it produced, were so very genuine. Life was simple but carried within it measurable qualities not found elsewhere as I have ventured on through it's pages. Time to reflect was spent well, as the train moved on through the night. I was better preparing myself for the unknown.

Upon returning to Deer Creek, we engaged in the same sort of training we had been doing before our leave to go home. Time quickly sped by for me. Scuttlebutt was out that we soon would be heading for the West Coast to pick up our ship.

We did not get any more liberties and I spent most of my free time at the PX or writing letters. I found the PX to be a good place to spend time, enjoying the lounge areas the Navy had provided for our comfort. This was a new adventure for me since I had very little exposure to the homey environment that the PX had created. More new adventures were just ahead and I was ready to experience them.

# 5

# OREGON BOUND

## All Aboard Again

One evening, in the latter part of January, we were told to make ready; we would be shipping out the next day. I got as much of my gear together as I could and was still able to sleep through the night.  Sure enough, the next morning we rolled our bedding in the hammock and marked it carefully with the tags they provided.  The hammock and bedding were stacked in neat piles and left to be shipped.  We carried our sea bag and ditty bag with us and formed our usual two lines out in front of the barracks. There was not a long wait before a line of Navy buses started showing up. We filed into the first available bus with all our gear in our laps and away we went. Excitement was in the air!  Most of us had never done very much traveling and the thought of a possible  long train ride was exhilarating!

News soon filtered down that we were going to Oregon. I had no idea of how we were to get to Oregon. We rode the buses to the railroad station in Washington D.C. There we unloaded and went into the train terminal to find the troop train to which we were assigned. We were told that we had some time on our hands, about four hours before departure. Several of the guys got pretty excited at this announcement. This meant that they could toss down a few beers. Those of us that did not drink stayed behind and watched the gear.

I still had a good farm appetite and spent a good deal of my waiting time eating. Hamburgers were still a novelty to this country boy. I discovered that ice cream stirred up into what they called a "shake" was another exciting adventure. I found that the time for departure went by very fast. The drinking shipmates started drifting back to the terminal, usually two by two. "Where is Gallagher?" I heard someone saying. Gallagher, had been appointed as my gunner's mate at Deer Creek. I felt a little responsible and concerned for him when I heard he was not there and with us leaving soon.

I moved out to the outer edge of the terminal and started looking for him. Sure enough, I found him wandering around, very drunk, but still able to walk. He saw me and started yelling, "Stroud, Stroud," in his Southern voice. He always had trouble correctly

146

pronouncing "Shrout." I was the only familiar face in the crowd to him. He grabbed hold of me and away we went, bobbing and weaving through the dense sea of travelers. We found our way back to where the crew was about to board the train.

The ride across America was my first east-to-west adventure, and as each mile of it came and went, I found myself more and more intrigued with this big majestic land we were freshly trained to defend. Along the way, word would be out that we were coming through and stopping in their fair town, so young ladies would be at the track side with their baskets of goodies. Doughnuts seemed to be the most common item. They were something that the girls could make themselves. As I would hang out the window of the railroad car and extend my hand for a delicious gift, I thought to myself, "This is great! I really like it!"

As we crossed through Indiana, my heart was very heavy. I could imagine my mom in the kitchen preparing breakfast for Dad. There was a good snow cover, or at least it looked so from the train window. Mom's way of frying ham to go along with the farm fresh eggs she always managed to have, moved through my thinking. I could almost smell the wonderful aroma. The Indiana farm house seemed so close, yet so far, to be a real part of what was going on there that day as the train journeyed on its way.

I found myself wondering if I would ever be a part of that good life again. I had been convinced by what I had heard in the sketchy war news before enlisting that not all service men would return. Boot camp did not add any more to my hopes of a safe return. We were told day after day that the enemy was going to be shooting at us. Time would prove that of course, but this country boy sure felt his pangs of nostalgia as we bumped along on the troop train across the state of Indiana. My memories of home were precious, and I remember as I gazed out the car window towards the roots of those memories, that I had some misgivings about being in the Navy.

The train sped on through the night across Illinois in a northwesterly direction. I remember the open prairie of the Dakotas and the vastness of Montana. I thought we never would get across it. Down the Columbia Gorge and on into Portland, Oregon, we made our way. On the morning of the third day we stopped on a siding that turned out to be in an area between the Williamette River and some empty appearing warehouse. We quickly moved outside the car, grabbed our hammock and bedroll gear that had been tossed in a large pile on the ground, then headed in a column of twos for the warehouse.

# The Great Northwest

The large warehouse proved to be quite comfortable. We were informed to go to the second floor that we could gain entrance to by outside wooden stairs. A long wide hall ran the full length of the second floor with several rooms on each side of the hall. The rooms were large with high ceilings and two rows of double bunks. My best recollection is that there were about fourteen double bunks in each room. I picked an empty bunk in the southeast corner room and stowed my gear on and about the bunk. We were told to show at a special muster at noon that same day on the first floor of the warehouse. There was a large open area that was used to muster in, or answer to roll call each morning.

The mess hall and galley made up the rest of the lower floor. Noon time came and we quickly answered to our names as called. Boatswain's Mate Onufer informed us that we were to muster each morning at eight at this very same location. It was very important that we be there, but the rest of the time we were on our own. Wow! Full time liberty had caught up with me! I was beginning to really like this Oregon assignment.

Not knowing anything about Portland and where we might find food, we ambled over to the mess hall for noon chow. The food was not so bad but I was anxious to explore the city of Portland. I told myself that I would do just that as soon as they told us we could go. After the noon chow, Boats told us, "You are on your own; behave and be sure to report for muster at eight sharp in the morning." Could I really believe my ears? This could be a lot of fun, I began to tell myself. I was ready to begin to find out what it was like to be a serviceman during wartime in a big city with plenty of time to explore its attractions.

**Newberry and Little standing on the landing leading to
our barracks warehouse home in Portland, Oregon
Note the mops in rack behind Newberry**

# Playtime - Portland

The very first thing I did after the informative first muster was to go with several of the guys to downtown Portland. To do this I found to be very simple. I did not realize just how close the warehouse-barracks was to all of the fun places to go in this big city. All I had to do was go out the south door of the barracks and over a few yards of empty lot and up past the side of a tavern that faced Burnside Avenue. Immediately to my right was the beginning of the picturesque Burnside Bridge that crossed the Williamette River.

The Williamette is a beautiful river that meanders in a northerly direction from the south end of Portland through the heart of the city and dumps all of its collected waters into the mighty Columbia River. Night and day for decades, the Williamette has managed to divide Portland's East from its West, a beautifully portrayed responsibility.

As I crossed the Burnside Bridge for the first time, I stopped in the middle of the bridge and gazed up and down the river. I was spellbound at the awesomeness of this creation of God's, and to have it so close to my bunk.

152

As I completed the crossing, I found myself gawking at the first of what Portland had to offer to servicemen. Very close to the bridge were more taverns and of all things, a theater that had live burlesque on its stage between movies. To someone from a small farming community, this really looked like "sin city." I had heard about such things that went on in the big city, but here it was, flaunting itself to little ol' me. I found myself thinking, "Man, this is pretty neat: a country boy walking around just as big as you please in one of the largest cities in the Northwest. Wait until I tell them about this back in my hometown in Indiana." The biggest excitement I would find in Akron would be a family-type movie at the Madrid, or peeking in the windows of the local tavern, watching the older guys play cards. I could see them drinking beer from their dark brown bottles and flipping their playing cards on the table.

The United States Army had a training center at Fort Lewis, Washington, north of Portland a hundred miles or so. During the peak time of World War II, the base provided lots of soldiers or "doggies," as we called them, that were looking for entertainment. They were everywhere in Portland. The soldiers arranged to ride the bus or train to Portland when they were able to secure passes. The only sailors in Portland were small groups such as ours picking up a small landing craft ship constructed in Portland. Talk about liberty privileges, we had it. I recall on the very first time in downtown Portland being encountered by a couple young ladies in a convertible. They pulled over to the curb alongside where I was walking, stopped their car, and wanted to know what I was doing and would I like to spend the evening with them. It hit me so fast, I just stared at them in disbelief. The girls looked like they probably had a lot of money and were very attractive. This was not what I was used to. I had heard that men were scarce but no way could I have imagined I would have been propositioned in this way. I gave them a weak "no thanks" and kept walking.

I visited all three of the USO establishments in Portland that evening. I had spent a lot of time with a ping-pong paddle in my hand back in Akron. I found that each USO had at least two ping-pong tables and one, the Catholic USO, had four. From that day on, I spent many hours over the next few weeks hammering the ball back and forth. I remember playing a sailor who said he was New York State champion. He was good! I believed him and managed to beat him before my stay in Portland concluded. There is one thing about ping-pong; if you play someone long enough you eventually learn all of their moves.

Each USO provided lots of goodies for us to eat. They had excellent sandwiches and all of the pie and milk we could consume. I thought I had found "Heaven" with all of this kindness available at my beck and call. I would skip going to the Navy mess at the barracks and wait until I could go  to one of the USOs and then I would really chow down on their delicious food selections.  I was beginning to enjoy the food of the world.  I missed my mom's table offerings but the new tastes of the outside world were starting to suit me just fine.


## Those Sailors and Women That Did

Some of my shipmates to be had other things in mind besides spending time in the USO.  Local bars and taverns provided an excellent place for them to make contact with  single women, but many times their evening of pleasure was with a married woman.  I would hear from different ones as they returned to the barracks about a certain woman they had met that was lonesome for her serviceman husband.  I could not believe what was happening.  My early childhood training included respect for other people, especially their spouse if they were married.  War time cast many of our men and women into situations that would have had little or no chance of occurring in peacetime.

Some evenings I would come back to the barracks early.  The building would be ever so quiet.  Hardly any

155

other person would be there.  Then about 10:00 pm, I would hear Michaels coming down the long barracks hall, singing in a loud voice some song that came to him in his inebriated condition.  He never got so drunk that he could not perform a task  taught each sailor in boot camp.  We were instructed that if we indulged in sex with a strange woman, we were to make use of a prophylactic medicine kit.  Each barracks had a dispenser or two  just for such occasions.  I can almost  hear the crackling sound of the paper wrapper from the kit as it was entwined about Michaels' most private part.  This was the last procedure to assist in containing the ointment he had so generously applied to his exposed body part.

He had made his early night stand with a nearby resident whom he had become acquainted with in a bar close to the barracks.  No need for him to go all the way downtown.  By the time he made his way to  where I was waiting and listening, he was ready to flop into his bunk.  He was out until I rolled him out for muster the next morning.   All of the liquor and evening activity he had engaged in had done him in.  I observed him on several occasions going through this same ritual.  Michaels was married and older by a few years.   I found myself wondering if I would ever become that callous.

I was learning in leaps and bounds about the world about me.  Several of the men in my crew were married, and most of the single guys had much more experience than I in the ways of the world. Somehow my small community back home had not demonstrated this lifestyle to me. I do not recall that I was worried or upset. I knew that I was prepared for whatever was tossed my way. Even though exacting details of what to expect were not knowledgeable to me, I never-the-less felt that the training and instruction that I had received from my parents would see me through just about anything.

When I returned one evening I found Fosburg in the head, sitting on the toilet, sicker than a dog, vomit all over himself and the floor. He moaned to me "Shrout, oh am I sick, I wish I could die!" I did not know what to do, realizing this was a case where a young man had experimented with too much drink and perhaps some of it bad stuff. I managed to give him some encouragement and scooted out of that mess to the protection of my bunk.

My only appearances at any of the taverns were at the one next to the barracks. I would go over on occasion and rescue a shipmate unable on his own to navigate the short distance back to the barracks. I did go often enough that as I would perch myself on a stool at the bar, the bartender on duty would slide a glass of milk down the bar to me. He knew me well enough to give me the right kind of drink. After all, I helped keep their good customers out of trouble and able to give them repeat business.

# SHROUT - AFTER the MUD

Our stay in Portland was short, spending six weeks in the converted warehouse barracks. The six weeks were used by our crew to have one giant-sized liberty. Our only assignment was to report for muster each morning at eight o'clock. There were mornings when even Boats was not there and Barron, coxswain third, called the roll. He never looked up to see who answered yo. There were many times we answered for someone who did not make it back in time, and no one seemed to mind. We were starting to jell as a crew in our looking out after one another.

Several of the crew became friends of women who invited them to their homes to stay for days at a time. It was on some of these occasions that we filled in at muster for them. I could understand why single guys would want to explore all of the avenues of life. My training at home made it difficult for me to understand why some of my married shipmates would feel justified to cheat on their wives. When we discussed the issue, they would simply say that we were at war and they did not know how long they would be alive. It made some sense, but I was still dealing with my mother's hard line teaching of what was right and wrong.

I spent a lot of time in downtown Portland at the USO's, finding them to be a place where I could feel safe. I could usually find something there that reminded me of a bit of home. The local Lions Club entertained our crew in the downtown Multnomah Hotel. Besides a nice lunch, they presented us with all kinds of table games for our use on the new ship we were about to commission. Portland has always had a special place in my memories over the years. Little did I know at that time that I would move my family to Portland to assume the position of Vice President of Finance for a private college. I still reside in Oregon.

# Commissioning of the 73

The **LCS (L)(3)73** was built by the Albina Engine and Machine Works of Portland, Oregon. Her keel was laid January 16, 1945. The letters LCS stand for Landing Craft Support. The (L) designates that it is the largest of US support craft ships. At the same time, it was one of the smallest sea going vessels. The Japanese called them "vest pocket destroyers." At a distance, the LCS did look like a destroyer.

Early on the morning of Monday, February 19, 1945, just 34 days after the start of ship construction, the entire crew left the barracks on Burnside Street with all personal gear. We loaded on Navy buses and headed for Pier five in the North Portland shipyard. There was a light mist of rain seeping through the thin, sleepy looking fog that tried to hide the outline of our future home. What a thrill it was to break through the cloak of nature and put foot on deck of our new ship for the very first time! The response our feet received from the hard steel deck seemed to have a warmth radiating through the soles of our shoes, welcoming each of us to our new vehicle of rest. The feel of strength that the hard steel portrayed assured us that our new home would also become our fortress of war.

We quickly stowed our gear in our assigned bunk locations. Mine was the upper, of three high, in hole number one. This put me just below the main deck on the starboard side of the bow. A manhole through the main deck was about eighteen inches from where my head rested on my pillow at night. I made quick note of the distinct advantage I had of an escape route just in case the compartment filled up with water or was on fire. If this were to happen, I could be the first one out.

The bunks were made of canvas, laced with line through grommets holding it taut between an aluminum frame. The size of the bunk was such that the average sailor's body fit snugly in the crater it formed when it was occupied. Later that evening, I discovered that when I would turn over, my shoulders would almost rub the large ventilation pipe that ran the full length of my bunk before disappearing into the neighboring bulkhead.

160

**Commissioning of the *USS L.C.S. (L) (3) 73***
**The 73 was 157 feet long with a 23 foot beam. Fully loaded, the ship displaced 395 tons and was driven by two groups of diesel engines called quads. Armament included three twin 40 mms, four single 20 mms, and a dozen Mark 7 rocket launchers.**

Each occupant of the hole was assigned a small half length locker, in which I found that I could easily get all of my earthly Navy issued possessions. Once gear was stowed, we reported to the main deck for commissioning ceremonies. We had dressed in our dress blues early that morning just for this situation.

At 0900 Naval time, Captain L.D. Whitgrove, representing the Commandant of the Thirteenth Naval District, ordered Lt. P.S. Carlton, USNR, Prospective Commanding Officer, to read his orders. Lt. Carlton read his orders and assumed command. The starboard watch was set with Ensign Russell E. Spencer, USNR, assigned to the first Officer of the Day watch. The ship was now placed in full commission. A muster roll of sixty-five enlisted men and a roster of six officers was prepared and forwarded to Bureau of Naval Personnel. The ship's Characteristic Card was sent to the CNO (Commander of Naval Operations). The Commissioning Party went ashore at 0912 Naval time. It was over! We were now official and this meant the crew of the **73** had picked up the weapons of war and were about to begin their part in the history of the United States of America and World War II.

Various local Portland suppliers delivered the first supplies to the docks. The first items were milk, eggs and some bakery goods. This all began to happen around 1010 Naval time. From the first supply items received, the cooks privileged to have the first watch in the galley were able to put together a lunch for the crew at 1200.

The first afternoon of our presence aboard our new home provided opportunity to work, carrying aboard various fruits and vegetables. It began to look like we were really going to eat "high on the hog." Colors (American flag) were taken down and anchor lights turned on at 1600. Night time was approaching and so was my very first experience of sleeping on-board the **73**.

We had our first real meal the first night aboard. Carriger and Rice both jumped in and turned out a meal that let the crew know that they could expect some great repasts in the days ahead. As I retired below deck at dusk, I began to explore the area assigned to me.

When we first came aboard that morning we did not have much time to check things out. My locker was small, not much bigger than my sea bag standing on end. With considerable rearrangement, I managed to get all items accessible and felt that I could function from it nicely. I spent the rest of the available time before lights out, becoming better acquainted with the guys that would become almost a part of me over the next several months, living in such close quarters.

As I listened to the steady hum of the air filtering system and tried to dismiss the pangs of anxiety that tried to slip into my thoughts, I would catch myself envisioning the scenes of home. I would let my thoughts slip away and I would start to wonder what it must be like in the cold of the night in the old farm house back home. I knew all too well just how cold February could be in Indiana. I was in a much milder climate in Oregon and felt very safe and cozy in my new abode.

The quiet barracks at boot camp were so different from the sounds of the ship as it seemed to breathe away through the night. This provided a sound barrier to hide the noise of my closely stashed shipmates as they rambled into slumber land, each in his own way. Sleep finally replaced the activities of the day, a day that perhaps was one of my most interesting thus far.

On Tuesday, Coxswain Barron flipped on the lights, and in a polite voice notified us, "Hit the decks, men, its reveille time." It was 0600. Not bad. I thought they might pull something and get us up earlier. I was starting to like ship duty, as I eased myself down from the upper bunk by carefully putting my left foot on a lower bunk across the way and then down to the deck. The two rows of bunks on my side of the hole were about two and one half feet apart.

I ran up the ladder that allowed us to exit our hole, trying to act as "old salt" as I could. The ladder was just that, almost straight up and you used the hand rail on each side for safety and speed. Emerging from my new found sleeping hole and about 15 feet ahead, was the hatch or entry way into the head. Entering the head, and inside to my right, were three small wash basins. Straight across from the hatch and under a port hole was a large tumbler type clothes washer. Turning to my left were two shower stalls without doors and across from them was the three position "john." All of the equipment used in maintaining good personal hygiene were housed in an area about twelve feet square.

Seawater was pumped from the port side of the ship and ran constantly from one end to the other of the half-moon shaped metal tank. The tank was about six feet long and had three sets of two boards, each shaped to fit the bottom side of the user. The water, after it had passed the length of the tank, exited the starboard side along with any deposits that might have been added by members of the enlisted crew. My mind went back to the old "three-holer" on the Shewman farm of my early Indiana days. I found out later the boards were quickly removable for a purpose other than cleaning. The first time I made my appearance to the head for seasick purposes I learned how easy the boards could be pitched aside. This allowed me, after falling on my knees, to hang my head over the side of the metal tank. I would be in a better position to dismiss the problem for which I had come there to be relieved.

That first morning I had plenty of time to do all of the necessary head chores. Not like boot camp days where we ran from one activity to the next. I went to the ship's mess (chow hall) and leisurely had a good breakfast of toast, eggs and bacon. I went back to my hole and spent a few minutes chewing the fat with several of the guys who now had become my hole mates.

Time went fast and soon we had to make ready for 0800 quarters. The enlisted men gathered on the main deck, stood at attention while colors were raised, and then answered "yo" to our names, as they were called. The ship's commissioned officers had taken their places during the ceremony on the next deck up, called the deck house. Some referred to this as the flag deck since most flag activity originated from this area. A large locker located on this deck stored the flags. They were arranged so they could be quickly attached to lines and hoisted upward from the locker.

The rest of the day was spent on work details, taking on what I thought to be huge quantities of supplies and stores to finish outfitting the ship. A partial but interesting list of supplies we loaded included 144 lbs. of butter, 70 lbs. of cheese, 2,584 lbs. of meat and 10 gallons of ice cream.

Each evening while in port, colors would be taken down and anchor lights turned on before dusk. A jack flag, similar to the union of the national ensign, was attached to the jack staff, a small vertical spar at the bow.

The next three days found us engaged in routines similar to what we did on Tuesday. More supplies had to be taken aboard, and I found myself wondering just where we would find more space to store all the items that came aboard. As I trudged back and forth around the deck house, up and down the ladders, opening this hatch and that, I was beginning to find myself getting more and more used to my new home.

On Saturday immediately after quarters, special sea detail was announced, starboard side. This meant that those who had been assigned special sea detail on the starboard side had to "turn to." Turn to was a Navy expression to get to work. This required about twelve seamen to work in small groups at each line holding the ship. Since I was on port side detail, I just watched to see how it was done. I felt very confident that I could handle this chore when called upon.

## SHROUT - AFTER the MUD

With lines properly stowed, some of us positioned ourselves by the rails on both sides and watched with admiration as our Skipper, Lt. Carlton, maneuvered us gracefully out of our port position and got the **73** underway. It was about 0815, and scuttlebutt had it that we were headed for the Interstate Terminals to take on ammunition.

The Interstate Terminals were an impressive looking dockside warehouse. It looked like to me that it was constructed from concrete. About twenty seamen went ashore as a work detail, and I remained aboard to actually store the ammo when the shore party brought it back to our ship. When we were through stuffing the various kinds of instruments of war in the appropriate storage areas, I looked over the shoulder of the quartermaster and read from his order sheets. I discovered that we had taken on 6,240 rounds of 40 mm ammunition; 8,820 rounds of 20 mm ammunition; 240 rockets; 4,500 rounds of .30 caliber; 3,600 rounds of .45 caliber and 4,000 rounds of .22 caliber ammunition.

Other miscellaneous items included signal projectiles, and a few shotgun shells. We were a floating powder keg! I started thinking about how much space on our small ship housed something explosive. It was incredible! Little did I know then how many close calls we would have in the oncoming days in having this supply of explosives put to test in various jars and jolts from sand bars, rocks, docks and some close calls with the enemy.

Sunday morning was spent lazing around. All the time I was hoping that Boats would not think of something for us to do. It was kind of nice to not do much on Sunday. We were underway again in the afternoon and took on 12,000 gallons of diesel fuel oil. We needed the assistance of a harbor pilot to get us to Richmond Oil who supplied the fuel from huge dock side storage tanks. Then we returned to the Interstate Terminal dock. It looked to me that we were now ready for sea and the chances of our involvement in the war grew by the hour.

While in Portland, we seemed to eat quite well. As a pie eater all of my life, it is easy for me to recall the delicious pies as they came aboard our ship. Crispi-Pie Company of Portland delivered fourteen pies each day to the **73**. I was usually around to observe this arrival and started looking forward with much anticipation to the appointed hour of their consumption. With a crew of seventy-one men, and if the pies were to be divided evenly, they would have to be cut in sixths. My mathematics told me there would be thirteen pieces left. I always wondered who got the extra pieces, but I never had the nerve to ask the cook.

When I awakened Monday morning, I expected to get the word that we would be underway in search of action. Instead, we cast off and went after fresh water. I had forgotten that we needed that important commodity. On that particular occasion we took on 6,500 gallons. This figured out that about ninety-one gallons of the water belonged to me.

The next three days were spent trying out various functions of the ship. Several times we would form special sea detail and cast off. The officers took turns working with the Skipper on the conn tower testing different maneuvering feats. It made sense to do this in free and easy water. The officers had to do a lot of testing of the compasses, which was called "compass compensation."

Tuesday saw our first official injury. Barron was treated for laceration of an index finger by Pharmacist's Mate Schoeller. He injured it while scraping paint. I found that from almost day one we would be scraping and painting the deck or other parts of the ship. This went on for as long as I was aboard. I wondered just how this injury would look in our deck logbook. In all of the war movies I had watched back home, entries in books of record only recorded injuries from heroic incidents.

I stopped trying to guess when we would be battle worthy. I told myself we would go soon enough and I sure did not want to forget anything we might need. Each day saw more supplies brought aboard. Seventy-one men do eat a lot. Regularly established inventories had to be maintained. Besides the usual 14 pies, I noted on Thursday that 200 loaves of bread came aboard. I thought to myself, that must mean we are leaving Portland. That was a lot of bread!

It was not Navy custom to keep the enlisted men advised of what was next. I was starting to find out that we had to wait and just see what came next. Meanwhile, Boats or Barron would usually find something that they would want some of us seamen to do. It might be a brass fitting that had started to take on a little tarnish look and would have to be polished. Even though the ship had just been commissioned, we could be found repainting a place or two on almost any given day, if it was not raining.

I started to become more familiar with some of my shipmates in the many hours of standing watch in small gun watch teams. The United States was at war and we had to have someone ready at all times, just in case something would happen. Much of our conversation moved in and about our families back home. I was learning who had brothers and who had sisters, and of course, if their sisters were good looking and their ages and etc.

We would stand watch around the outer edge of the gun mount in the gun tub of the 40 mm just forward of the wheel house. This was the gun that I was assigned to for general quarters. The location of this gun tub had the best all around view of what was going on. The only place perhaps better would be the conning tower, generally referred to as the "conn." Unless you were an officer or duty signalman, the conn was off limits to enlisted men.

Friday morning March 2, 1945, found us casting off all lines at 0800 and getting underway with all main engines running at various speeds conforming to channel regulations. Wow, we were off! We had been waiting for this moment for several days. I could really tell that the excitement of the unknown adventure before us was racing through each one's mind. A Lt. Logan with the U.S. Coast Guard was on-board acting as our pilot. He knew where all of the snags, bars, and other ship pitfalls were located and assisted our Skipper in getting the **73** around them.

Steaming in a northerly direction in company with the *101* and the *102*, we found ourselves entering the main part of the Columbia River, heading northwest towards Astoria. As we turned into the Columbia, the **73** became the middle ship as we moved up the river. What excitement! I remember standing forward on our ship allowing the wind to blow about me as we moved rapidly through the river water.

172

All of the memories I had of the preparational training in boot camp and in Fort Pierce gunnery school seemed to rush into my most inner thoughts. These thoughts seemed to fuel the anticipation of what the tomorrows might bring.    After all, some of these new experiences could be just around the turn in the mighty Columbia that lay before us.  Each breath, each moment, each new horizon beckoned to me as I savored the rich river water air in my dry land seasoned lungs.  I was a long way from the farm in Indiana and was now riding the bow of something that was a far cry from the front of Dad's bundle rack wagon.

All of my engrossment in the then and now was abruptly interrupted by the general quarters alarm horn as it started to blast loudly.  I noticed the time; it was 1121.  I started  to wonder if this would disturb our noon chow call that we had become used to at 1130 each day  aboard our new ship.  It turned out that this was the officers' way of getting us together for exercise.  We did a series of jumping jacks, a few push ups, and secured from general quarters just in time for noon chow.  It was just a few minutes later than the usual time.

During chow I noticed that my appetite had not been bothered by the motion of the ship in the water.  I had a good friend who told me before I left home that sometimes trying to eat while aboard ship was very difficult.  He said it was like swallowing a piece of greasy pork chop with a string tied around it, and then pulling at the string ever once in a while.   We were in relatively calm waters, but my day was yet to come.

I thought the trip up the Columbia was exciting.   I got to see both sides of the river from a very good vantage point.   The state of Washington was on the starboard and Oregon on the port side.   We arrived at the Naval Station in Astoria and moored portside to Pier # 2, berth # 7 .

The arrival time was officially logged in as 1558. Over the ship's public address system came the announcement from Ensign Spencer, "There will not be any shore leave for anyone tonight.   Make sure you stay aboard.   In case some of you do not understand, there already has been a gangway watch established.   He is armed and is instructed to shoot if necessary."   Man, I started to feel a little frightened over that comment.   If the person on gangway watch did not have anymore knowledge than I did about the pistol in his holster, we could all be in big trouble. Later, when I was assigned to relieve the watch, I learned that the ,45 caliber Colt automatic pistol did not have a clip in it.   Good 'ol Mr. Spencer was joshing us!

We spent the first night officially aboard  ship tied to the dock in Astoria, Oregon.   We were not bouncing up and down on the Pacific Ocean as I had imagined. I found it quite intriguing to look across the dock area and up into the homes of the local citizens. War did not seem close. We could almost feel like we were on an unrelated military experience, as the guest of some rich dude that had a ship like this one on his list of assets. I wrote a few letters to the family back home and hit the sack early. As dreamland engulfed my being, I remember thinking of the homes on the hills of Astoria and tried to equate them to what it might be like back at my Indiana home.

At 0750 quarters was piped over the loud speakers. A boatswain's pipe is blown by the duty boatswain giving a variety of different orders or commands to the seamen. Everyone was accounted for in the muster after we had spent our first night in port aboard our new ship. Colors were hoisted and we secured from quarters. I could not see much activity on the dock.

Our ship did not stand up very high. I could see about a half dozen other smaller type ships also moored in the general area. I would not call Astoria a city that looked much like a Navy town. It appeared to be a quiet, sleepy small town, perched on the edge of America awaiting the unknown. The inhabitants knew all too well that they could be disturbed very quickly by the enemy who lived just across the water that caressed Astoria's shores. They were the closest to the enemy, and in the apparent laid back position the community seemed to be in, could be quite vulnerable.

## San Diego By Water

All lines were cast off at 1058 with a new pilot aboard, a Commander Anderson of the U.S. Coast Guard of Astoria. We continued the same order of ships in column as the day before and headed for San Diego, California, with Captain Carlson on the con. I really did not know it would turn out to be San Diego until later in the afternoon, when the scuttlebutt finally drifted down to the enlisted men.

As we left the protection of the jetty walls and entered the Pacific Ocean, the **73** had its first real for goodness shakedown cruise. I thought the swells we encountered would tear us apart at the seams. Some of the crew got a little sick and had to visit the head to make use of the removable seats. It was not considered the proper thing to use the area immediately off the ship's rail to relieve one's previous chow material. We were told that the head would be more appropriate. I did not seem to be bothered too much by the ship's reaction to the swells of the sea, and hoped this was to be a sign that maybe I could ride out future rough seas without becoming too

176

sea sick.  I told myself that this was all in the mind and that I would do my best to not become seasick.

We continued all day, changing formation order, executing various maneuvers,  with the officers again getting a chance to feel the awesome  reality of commanding a ship.  The bad guys were across the water to our starboard, and we needed to be ready for them.  We all knew that we needed to practice as much as we could.  An encounter with the Japanese meant we would find out what war really was all about.  Each, in his own way, wanted to get involved in the fighting, but yet something within us caused us to think that we would just as soon delay it from happening for a little longer.

Hager, our radar man, picked up our first unidentified object on radar at 2320.  Five minutes later the object disappeared from the radar scope.  I was asleep below deck and did not know this happened.  We were informed at chow the next morning.  For all we knew, it could have been a Japanese destroyer.  We had heard rumors that the Japs were sneaking in close to the American western shore from time to time.  All of the crew knew we could not be too careful.

Five days were spent moving in a southerly course along the western coastline of the United States.  For the most part we could not see the shoreline as we moved

177

steadily through the mighty Pacific. We speculated at times that we were pretty sure we saw the San Francisco skyline. I was starting to get the all alone feeling of what it was probably going to be like when we really headed west.

March 7 found the **73** and other sister ships standing in to the San Diego harbor executing various courses and speeds conforming to channel regulations. We finally moored to *LCS(L)(3)93*. Liberty was almost immediately announced for the starboard watch side. The enlisted men were divided into two groups, a starboard side and a port side. Each man's location was determined by the side of the ship from which he had been designated to abandon ship. I had been assigned to the port side and knew exactly just what to do if and when we were given "abandon ship" orders. We practiced this several times before we left the security of the Portland dock.

Shopoff reported on-board shortly after midnight that he was injured by a Navy jeep on the San Diego Naval base at 0045. He had been treated at the base hospital for superficial cuts and bruises. Again I was sleeping below deck and heard nothing of the excitement until morning chow. I was beginning to learn that a lot of things could happen after I let my head hit the pillow. Shopoff had been with me since boot camp. He was also from Indiana, and we Hoosiers wanted to stick together.

## SHROUT - AFTER the MUD

The next evening port side had liberty. I was ready to see San Diego and find out what excitement it had to offer this farm boy. I carefully put on my dress blues, shined my shoes, and did my best in tying the square knot in my neckerchief. Tiny and Morris went with me on this first outing into greater San Diego. I really had not spent much time in the city of Chicago, other than hurriedly passing through from train to train while at boot camp. Portland had looked big to me, but the easy flow and laid back temperament of Portland's residents probably helped me make the adjustment from the country to the big city.

We caught a city bus at a stop not too far from the main gate to the Navy base. There was a sign in a little box over the driver's windshield that said "Downtown." That was where we wanted to go. Morris was from Michigan and Tiny came from upper New York. What a diverse looking threesome we must have presented to the local residents. Our beginnings in life must have surely shown itself in our demeanor; a farm boy from Indiana, half of a twin set of boys from Dearborn, Michigan, and this huge muscle-bulging, Atlas-looking blond German from Buffalo, New York. We did manage to stay out of trouble. I don't remember either of my two shipmates drinking any liquid spirits. We had the pleasure of sitting down and being waited upon in what looked like to me to be the world's biggest restaurant. It sure was nice to have a good looking young lady take our orders and bring our

179

food to us. What a change of pace from regular Navy life! We decided to go to a movie and then back to the ship.

The next morning at muster, Hennessy and Carriger did not respond to their names as called. They were marked as AWOL. We cast off all lines at 0933 and started our usual practicing in the large bay area. I kept wondering what was going to happen to Hennessy and Carriger. Hennessy was needed below deck in the engine room to help make all of the delicate maneuvers we were doing, and I just knew we would have a bad experience in the chow line, because I was convinced that Carriger was becoming a good cook. Not like Mom's of course, but he could do a a fair job. Now he was gone. Was he lost? Scuttlebutt started moving about the ship that the two of them had become drunk and that the Navy Shore Patrol had probably picked them up. What if we headed out to the front line with them not on-board? These were all new situations and questions in many of our minds. I quickly dismissed the thoughts and decided that they were adults and would have to take care of themselves.

Meanwhile we began taking on more stores. I thought the supply list was interesting and almost unbelievable. It indicated that we took on 50 pounds of bread, 141 pounds of oranges, 57 pounds of tomatoes, 116 pounds of lettuce, 36 pounds of apples, 80 pounds of apple sauce, 904 pounds of tomato catsup, 155 pounds of cherries, 78 pounds of chili, 150 pounds of coffee, 8 quarts of vanilla flavoring, 122 pounds of fruit cocktail, 78 pounds of gelatin, 261 pounds of evaporated milk, 135 pounds mince-meat, 12 gallons vegetable oil, 174 pounds of peaches, 158 pounds of pears, 162 pounds of pineapple juice, 152 pounds of sliced pineapple, 40 pound of dried spaghetti, 27 pounds of shredded wheat, 60 pounds of cookies, and 24 pounds of crackers. There were 74 pounds spinach, 400 pounds of sugar, 57 pounds of tomatoes, 108 pounds of tomato juice, 81 pounds of tomato paste, 95 pounds of tomato puree, 90 pound of onions, 1000 pounds Irish potatoes, 60 dozen eggs, 108 pounds pork loin, 122 pounds of sausage, 47 pounds bacon, 60 pounds butter, 100 pounds of cabbage, 50 pounds of carrots, 70 pounds of celery, 64 pounds of grapefruit, 75 pounds of lemons, and 4 gallons of horseradish. I don't ever remember putting horseradish on anything on the farm. This was a new item for me. When I tried some, I immediately wondered why we needed 4 gallons.

March 21st saw the return of Hennessy and Carriger under guard by the Navy shore patrol. They had been AWOL for twelve days. These were my shipmates. I could not look upon them the same as someone stealing chickens back home and under guard by our county sheriff. I was being introduced to another part of what was out there in the big old world. A week later, both men were given punishment under a Captain's Mast. Pfeiffer also appeared before them because of insubordination. He was one of our older men and it was harder for him to take orders. The Navy had a way of getting close to the core of problems. They issued punishment that hit home. In these cases, no liberties for awhile for these men. Staying aboard ship all of the time was real punishment when you knew your buddies were out on shore having fun.

The last part of March and the first part of April saw us busy everyday practicing some kind of exercise that might help us later in combat. We went out in the Pacific away from San Diego and did our maneuvers. At night we would drop anchor at either San Nicolas or San Clemente Islands. Both islands were several miles off the coast and were U.S. Military Reservations. We tried out all of the guns aboard, making firing runs on San Nicolas Island. Every kind of maneuver was made. All of this sort of thing made us more prepared for what was to come.

**Lt. Carlton and Chief Boatswain Mate Onufer
standing on dock in front of
author's 40 mm battle station**

Saturday morning, March 24, saw the exchange of pharmacist's mates. Moyer reported aboard and Schoeller left for some other duty. I liked Moyer; he was a nice quiet sort of a fellow. I was convinced that if I ever became sick, his bedside manner would be just fine. One of his first recorded assignments was to condemn eighty loaves of bread. Bread does not keep long on dry land, however, on-board a ship even less time before it starts to mold. The Captain ordered the bread to be tossed overboard. Fish in the harbor sure had a feast that day.

There were other *LCS's* participating in the same kind of exercises. They included the *74, 96, 101, 102, 103, 104*, and the *130*. We poured huge quantities of lead into the shores and sides of the small cliffs of San Nicolas Island. I wondered what the cliffs would be like to poke and probe around through in years to come. During one of our exercises, the *102* and the *103* collided with no apparent damage. We were pulling some fancy maneuvers. This was what it might be like someday. We had to be good at executing all of the moves to stay safe.

We made running passes and commenced strafing fire on the beaches. We would stand by, secured from firing the 40 mm I was on, don our special glasses and wait for the crew of the forward 40 mm to fire the anti-personnel rockets. The launchers were immediately below my gun tub. We needed the glasses to protect our eyes from all of the flying ballistics.

We used the beaches of Pyramid Head on San Clemente Island when we were firing rockets. It was pretty scary when the rockets were fired. There were ten 4.5 inch Mark 7 launchers, each loaded with twelve anti-personnel rockets. They could all be discharged in just a few seconds. The air had a foul smell as it rose along with the small fragments of ballistics. When we fired the rockets, I would be standing next to the magazine of the port side 40 mm, about six feet away from the muzzles of the rocket launchers. The fourth of July back in Indiana was never quite like this.

Thursday, March 29, saw the **73** in dry dock. We had to unload all of the ammunition on-board. Otherwise, if we were to have a fire while repairs were underway, it would be a disaster. The propeller shaft bearings were repacked. I thought this to be unnecessary, but the Navy wanted us to leave the states in as good condition as possible.

Wednesday, April 4, two men were AWOL from the last evening's liberty. They were Gertz and Hansen. We received five new shipmates this day. They were Oliver, Heikkimen, Steinberger, Byl and Gates. Something must

185

be going to happen soon. We were filling up our crew. Gertz and Hansen returned Thursday after being absent a period of thirty-eight hours and six minutes. I knew they would be have to answer later to the Captain.

While our ship was having repairs made in dry dock, I lucked out and received a forty-eight hour pass. It was late afternoon when the pass was issued to me. I had asked around the crew for directions of the best way to go to Los Angeles. My brother, Irvin and his wife, Dorothy, had recently moved to that area as associate ministers in a church. Chief Petty Officer Dick was from California. He suggested that I take the "A Train." I did just that and it was a pleasurable ride up the coast. Brother Irvin met the train and I had an enjoyable two days in Los Angeles.

I spent the next few hours having lots of fun eating out at what I thought were fancy restaurants. My brother knew that I had little if not any experience in partaking of what the nice eateries had to offer. We visited a couple live radio broadcasts which I found to be very interesting. I was lucky to have a radio that worked when living on the farm. Here I was watching it all happen. It was fascinating!

I went to church with my brother and his wife on Sunday and rode the train back to San Diego and the bus back out to the Naval base.

186

**Ensign Anderson, gunnery officer of the 73**

**Author - starting to look like an "old salt" on liberty**

# 6.

# ADIEU - AMERICA

## Pearl Bound

We continued to stock our ship with stores and completely filled our ammunition magazines. Every day or so we would top out our water supply and supply of fuel. Wednesday, April 11, all lines were cast off one final time. We were underway for Pearl Harbor with the *101, 102* and the *130.* This was one time the Skipper shared with his crew what was ahead. He came on the ship's intercom, and in very assuring words told us that he thought that we were ready for battle. He told us that we should keep the almighty God in our thoughts and to not be ashamed to say a prayer every once in a while for our ship and its crew's safety. We heard a rumor that the Skipper had one ship shot out from under him at Salerno, and we all felt that he pretty well knew what he was talking about.

189

With the knowledge that we were on our way to Pearl Harbor, I could see some of my shipmates, myself included, beginning to find excuses to stand on the fantail of our ship, gazing longingly eastward at the slowly disappearing shoreline of America. In serious times like this, it seemed right not to have a heavy-duty assignment at that moment. It was time for us to think and reflect to ourselves just who we were and what we were leaving behind. Most of us were wondering if we would see those special people again. I had called back to my Akron home the night before. I remember saying to my mother, " Listen good to my voice, it will probably be a long time before you hear it again." Those last words to Mom have haunted me for decades. Little did I know that would be the last time she would hear my voice or I, hers. Mom died before I returned to the States.

As the afternoon started to become night, our small convoy of four ships disappeared over the horizon--the same western horizon that Americans gazed upon. We were heading west towards Hawaii and the unknown of what the Pacific might flush up in front of us. Our forward horizon vision was limited to only the three other ships in our convoy. There was so much water that I began to wonder just how battle effective our small ship and the three others could be in an emergency. The Pacific is so overpowering when there are only four small ships bouncing along at about thirteen miles per hour.

April 13, Friday morning at 0805, we dipped the National Ensign in honor of President Roosevelt's death. We were in awe at the passing of our commander-in-chief and knew little of what to expect. Hardly anyone had heard of our new President, Harry Truman. Everything stayed the same aboard the **73**. We kept our course 259 reading and maintained our speed of eleven knots. We all knew we must maintain our vigilance, for we were on our way to war. Whatever that turned out to be, we would handle it. I would remember this day as the day we dipped our flag and set our ship's clocks back one hour.

Each day was almost the same as the day before. We made a course change to a 255 reading. The chow menu would change. The sea was good. I was beginning to get used to the gentle roll and toss of our ship as we pressed forward in the wake of the 101, our appointed flag ship. Forty hours later after the last course change, we made another course change to reading 251. I marveled at how we could go in the exact same direction hour after hour and day after day. The America I loved was becoming a long way from me. Even at standard speed or eleven knots, we were leaving the security of home all too quickly. All of us were becoming more and more aware of the enemy and of the danger they presented.

The routine repeated itself for the next four days. The same course maintained and good weather prevailed. One day a Captain's Mast was held. It seems the Navy would not forget that some of the crew had been AWOL a few hours in the states. Hansen and Gertz were sentenced to three days of bread and water, 38 hours extra duty, and no future liberties until further notice. I couldn't see where doing without liberty was going to hurt much, with us out in the middle of the Pacific. However, bread and water did not sound too swift to me. I was used to at least having gravy on my bread.

April 20, 1945 at 1428, we entered Pearl Harbor and moored portside to the 72 at mooring buoy six in West Loch. All of the many days of patiently watching the horizon and declaring that it never changed or that we were never going to get to Pearl Harbor had now become fruitfully real.

I looked at the water in the harbor and tried to imagine what it must have been like on that Sunday morning, December 7, 1941. Here we were, three plus years later, the war still all about us in the Pacific, and we were gliding over sunken ships, planes, and bodies of our fallen servicemen. It was becoming apparent that we were becoming hardened to the evidences of war. Most of us were gazing out into this harbor water and were wondering what the cook was going to serve for noon mess.

192

Sunday, April 22, our first ship's yeoman came aboard. Scollin, Yeoman Second Class, reported for duty. Two days later, Strucely, Seaman second class, reported aboard for duty. Strucely, a signalman striker, spent a lot of time with me, teaching me semaphore. We would signal back and forth when he was on the conn on duty and with nothing much to do. Strucely was a quiet sort of sailor from Texas. I found myself spending a lot of leisure time with him.

More than three weeks were spent in Pearl Harbor. I was sent to gas warfare school, located on the main Naval base, for a two day refresher course. A small boat would come by and pick me up each day and bring me back in late afternoon. I was designated as the one to keep abreast of the latest tactics the enemy might use.

One day we pulled anchor and moved our ship out of West Loc and anchored off a repair pier that was just a few yards from Waikiki Beach. Some of the crew jumped over the side and swam to a buoy that lay a short distance off our starboard side. They would hold on to the buoy, catch their breath and then swim back to the **73**. I thought this looked like fun.

I went below to put on my swim trunks and came back topside. The deck was empty of crew and no one was in the water at that moment. I did a dangerous thing, as I jumped in and started swimming for the buoy. Dangerous thing number two was executed when, instead of pausing at the buoy for a few moments for rest, I just tapped it and started back to the ship. As I exhausted the distance between the buoy and the ship, I became more and more weary. Glancing up towards the **73**, I saw no one on deck. I did some serious thinking at that time. I could see my short life pass in front of me, but I was determined that I would make it to the ship.

Finally, I made it to the ladder that was hanging down to the water's edge. Hanging on for dear life, I rested for several minutes. I barely managed to pull myself up the ladder and crawl over the edge of the deck. Man, did the ship's deck ever look good! I decided right then and there that I never would do that foolish trick again. Someone should have been swimming with me or at least have some one ready on the deck that could have given assistance when they saw my plight.

We had lots of chances for liberty in Honolulu. Liberty boats, sometimes a LCVP, would make their runs among the ships at anchor in West Loc and take us ashore. The liberty boat would wind about through the ships, crossing over many areas that contained sunken debris from the results of that certain "day of infamy." The liberty boat would deposit us on shore close to a small train station.

194

When we wanted to go into Honolulu, we had to catch a narrow gauge-type train. The passenger car had open glassless windows. Lots of air blew through our hair as we puffed along through the fields of rural Hawaii, with sugar cane on one side and pineapples on the other. This seemed so strange to this Indiana farm boy. No corn or alfalfa fields were to be found.

The weather was warm and very pleasant, unusual weather for me to experience in April. I liked that part of it. The excitement of riding a small train into the unknown city of new adventures and historic sites was tremendous. I found this to be another great experience that I was recording for my memory to draw upon later.

Downtown Honolulu was what I had imagined the Orient to be like. Everywhere I looked were uniformed sailors. The local citizenry looked very much Asian. My only reference to this would have to be from pictures I had seen in the Akron Public Library, or a few real Asians I had seen on the streets during the short stay in Portland, Oregon. Before I left the farm, I do not recall ever seeing an Asian.

It was haircut time. I entered a barber shop located on what appeared to me to be the main street, which was called King Street. I looked around the barber shop and noted it contained four chairs. One chair was open and

195

the attending barber beckoned me to his chair. As I looked him up and down, I was sure that he had to be of the same descent to that of our enemy. With some hesitance, I climbed into his chair. I conjured up all kinds of thoughts while he finished my haircut with a nice close shave, using a very sharp-looking straight razor, as he went in about and around my ears. No problem, I received a very fine haircut. I gave him a quarter and left his shop chalking up my first "close shave" in the new world at war to which I was rapidly being introduced.

Liberty time in Honolulu also meant visiting the Royal Hawaiian Hotel. One would never guess what peace and serenity enveloped the area around the Royal Hawaiian. I visited the area a few years prior to this writing and found it to be one of the busiest places in the world. Not so during World War ll. As I walked the beach, I would see many sailors, and some would be with girlfriends with whom they had managed to become acquainted. Basking in the warm sun on the wide open beaches around the hotel was a popular past time. All of us would eat out every chance we could get. I always seemed to have enough money to pay for it.

Several times we would get aboard the liberty launch bound for Honolulu, only we would persuade the coxswain to veer out of his course to a small dock nestled amid the cane fields. I never did find out what use the dock had except for maybe moving the cane from the fields to other points. We had discovered that we could walk a short distance, perhaps just short of a mile and find ourselves in the sleepy little village of Waipio. The weather was always great. We found ourselves, at least part of the time, just relaxing on the green grass in the large yard in front of the city hall. There was a small USO where I had many wonderful times playing ping-pong and partaking of some of the great food that they offered to us. A cozy, quaint atmosphere seemed to be a little more acceptable to this country boy than all of the hustle and bustle of downtown Honolulu.

## Church in the Pacific

Just before noon on Wednesday, May 9, 1945, I was sitting on the fantail of the ship reading my small copy of **The New Testament** that the Gideons had given each of us back in Portland, Oregon. I was not aware that the Skipper stood behind me for several minutes observing my intense meditation. Later, over the ship's public address system, I was summoned to the Captain's stateroom. What had I done? I nervously approached the Skipper's stateroom and found him waiting in the doorway. "Come on in, Shrout," he said in a warm soft Southern voice. "Have a seat. I want to discuss something with you," he told me." I sat down in an empty chair, not knowing just what was around the corner for me. "Shrout, now that we are approaching possible enemy waters, more than ever we need someone to be our ship's Chaplain," he explained. Continuing in his soft Southern voice, he again said, "Normally, the Executive Officer fills this spot, but our Exec does not care to. Would you act as our Chaplain? I watched you for several minutes, and I could tell that you were indeed not faking it but serious about what you were doing. I need such a man right now," he said. I gulped a couple times and quickly said, "Yes sir, I would be glad to do it." "Whatever you need and whoever you need to assist you, let me know," the Captain told me. "Lets start next Sunday with a service in the chow hall and I will be there," the Skipper reassured me. "Thank you, sir," I told him, then saluted and left his stateroom with my heart all a flutter. I had never imagined, not even in my wildest dreams, that something like this could be happening to me.

I had a few days to think about what I wanted to say on that first Sunday. I wondered what my mom would think about all of this. I even thought about my former Sunday School teacher, Marion Higgins, and what she would have to say about the new assignment given to one of her students.

I went below and shared with some of my shipmates what the Skipper wanted me to do. Fritts told me he had seen the Skipper standing behind me from his position on the flag deck. I began to ask myself, how could something like this and as important as this, be assigned to me. I had no real experience in dealing with teaching devotional and spiritual things, especially to fellow servicemen. My close friends reassured me I could handle it and they would help.

It seemed to be appropriate that we have a church service the last Sunday in U.S. waters. Sunday evening, 1700, May 13, 1945, some of us met in the chow hall just prior to evening chow. Was I ever surprised! Coxswain Barron had made a small cross with electric lights. Fritts and Kloss said they were prepared to sing a couple of duets. The Skipper was sitting on the front row. With knees knocking and my heart pounding, I stepped to the front of the group.

I had let many ideas run through my mind as to what to say. Can you imagine what must have been going through some of my shipmates' minds? "What can Shrout tell us that would be pertinent and helpful to us?" they must have wondered. I asked the crew to sing a verse of "Amazing Grace" and another from "The Old Rugged Cross." I felt comfortable in leading these, thinking most of them would surely know them. And they did. I was really surprised at how intent they were singing and also what good voices they had.

Some of the thoughts I recall giving to them were: let us have faith that right makes might, and in that faith, let us dare to the end to do our duty as we understand it. l was quoting something that I had read President Lincoln had said. I instructed them that self-preservation is the first law of life, but it must operate selflessly. I also told them that when you face the light, the shadow is always behind you. I encouraged them to be strong and of a good courage, for the Lord thy God would be with them, no matter where they went or whatever happened. Fritts and Kloss sang all four verses of "Just a Closer Walk With Thee," and I said a short prayer and that was it. The **73** had experienced its first church service.

# Westward To the Front

May 15, 1945, we cast off all ship lines at 1420 and were underway with Captain Carlton on the conn and heading for someplace. We followed the 72 out through the harbor and past the harbor nets. As we straightened our course, I could tell that we were heading southwest towards what I knew all too well was the position of our enemy, the Japanese. Now we were soon going to be doing what we had been trained to do; find the enemy and destroy them. It took a lot of zigging and zagging to clear the harbor. There were many ships at anchor awaiting their own particular orders. Nets were below the water's surface to ward off any possible submarine intrusion. The Skipper of the 72, our command or flag ship, had the necessary charts and know-how to get us through. As soon as we had made all of the adjustments for leaving and had finally cleared the area of Pearl Harbor, we set our course to 255.

*The LCS (L) (3) 73*
*Headed out, loaded and ready for action*

From the moment we cast off lines, starboard watch was set. We would be operating under "condition three." This meant that the starboard side or one half of the ship would be subject to duty, until the next regular watch change of 1600. From that point on, the watch would be relieved every four hours. In this case, the port side was to relieve the starboard watch fifteen minutes prior to 2000. I was assigned to the port side watch.

Each watch section was divided into divisions. In condition one or general quarters, all men were at some station. Under condition two, or when general quarters is eminent, half of the ship's crew would be on duty. Condition three was the normal cruising situation and usually only a third were assigned posts. When we were in port, a smaller duty group was required.

During the daylight hours, and if not on special duty, I could expect to be working at some task usually up on deck assigned by our Chief Boatswain's mate or one of our two coxswains. After evening chow, we were called to general quarters and found it to be another time do some exercising. Our skipper wanted us to stay in shape and be ready for any emergency.

On through the night the **73** and its three other LCS buddy ships plowed the waters of the Pacific. It was a little difficult to get to sleep the first night away from the most western shore of America. All of my short life I had grown to respect the safety and protection of my country. Now, my future depended on my shipmates, and of course, my ability to jell with them and to learn to depend on our training skills for our safety. Sleep finally took command of our weary and worrying bodies. The light of morning came as a welcome beacon. Coxswain Barron walked among our bunks at 0600 advising us to "Hit the deck."

I quickly climbed the ladder from hole number one and popped through the hatch near the top of the ladder to the port side of the main deck. The sea was reasonably quiet and the good ol' **73** was still moving ahead at standard speed or about ten and one-half knots. As I gazed both port and starboard, I could see nothing but water. The horizon that encircled us seemed so far from us, yet in many ways I felt as though I could reach out and touch it. The part of me that told me that I was starting to think that I was an old salt allowed me to devour morning chow with an unusually good appetite. I was somewhere in the Pacific heading for war and the youth in me was surfacing. I was eager to see what it was like to meet the enemy.

I watched others of the crew as they joined me at the rail. They seemed to have the same far away look on their faces as they in turn evaluated the scene presented to them. Looking out into the vast Pacific and seeing only water and no other forms of life is a lonesome feeling. We were all abruptly interrupted with the sound of general quarters at 1050. We could see a ship on the horizon. We stood anxiously by our stations. I had taken the cover off of the twin forty magazine that I was assigned to  man. I was ready to stuff the clips of 40 mm rounds into my side of the gun and get the show on the road.  But the ship turned out to be one of our own, and we secured thirty minutes later from our first real general quarters.

Carter, who was my first loading companion on the other half of our twin forty, helped me put the cover back on our double headed magazine. This procedure  repeated itself over and over.  Many general quarters would be sounded. In fact, one was sounded the same evening at 1845 and turned out to be nothing that we could see from our position. We secured at 1955.  We were starting to get the routine down quite well.

Thursday, May 17, we were told to set our watches and clocks back one hour to plus eleven time zone. I was beginning to think that the entire crew was as jumpy as I was.  We logged three general quarters alarms this day. They proved to be our own shipping.  I suppose we were causing them to sound their alarms also.  In spite of all of the interruptions from racing to our general quarters stations,  we plowed on and on, all day and all night, through the mighty Pacific.  I began to wonder if this big ocean had another side to it. All I could see was water and more water. I managed to get a full night's sleep without any general quarters interruptions. The gentle roll and toss of our ship, as it cut through the relatively smooth ocean surf, was beginning to cause my body to relax and my mind to think of past pleasant times.

The next morning, the Captain talked to us over the loud speakers and informed us we were on our way to Eniwetok in the Marshall Islands, and that it would take us eleven days from Pearl Harbor. At last we knew something of what we were about. There was fat chance that we could tell anyone where we were going. We were at sea and no way to communicate with anyone, other than our shipmates.

During the day of Thursday, May 17, 1945, general quarters was summoned three times. Each time found ships on the horizon that did not respond to our identification testing. This was because some were of older shipping and did not have answering devices on-board. We had to wait it out and check visually to make sure they were not those of the enemy. A lot of my viewing time of the Pacific was from my gun tub position.

After we secured from each general quarters, I found lots of time to stand at the rail and watch. The blue Pacific waters would kick up and flow past us into the wash of the wake we were creating, as we moved through the month of May. I would learn that many times we would be falsely alerted to potential danger from unidentified "pips" on the radar screen.

**Radarman Hager with the PPI scope behind him**
**This is the place the author reported for**
**battle station condition two**

206

Friday midnight watch found me joining radarman Hager, sharing our first official radar watch aboard the **73**. We were starting a condition two watch situation. The flag ship had notified us that the enemy could be in these waters, so we must take extra precautions. My watch assignment was to watch the PPI scope (plan-position indicator). The scope, or tube, was about 14 inches in circumference. A sweeping ray of light rebounding from the radar antenna, high on the ship's mast, kept going round and round the surface of the tube. As the light ray passed over an object, it caused a blurb or smudge to appear on the scope. The unidentified object became a target classification until we determined whether it was friend or foe. We had equipment on the mast that gave us this information. It was referred to as IFF (identification, friend or foe).

We secured the radar watch at 0400, but had no more than hit the sack when we were awakened to another general quarters at 0522. It again proved to be nothing dangerous and was secured at 0610, just in time for morning chow. With a night of jitters and stress, it was difficult to enjoy the cook's scrambled eggs and bacon, though just as tasty as they had been in the days before. Was this how it was going to be on a daily basis?

Our heading out of Pearl Harbor was 255T. It was interesting to discover we never changed our headings much, only a degree up or down from the previous heading. On the sixth day out of Pearl Harbor we changed to a 245T heading. I could almost feel the change as I stood on the deck and looked forward as the **73** moved through the night.

I observed that general quarters alarms were becoming more regular. We were starting to experience them as much as three times a day. I think that each of us was as alert as we could be when they sounded. We jumped out of our sacks and hit the deck running. We did not need much convincing that it was possible for anyone of these alerts to end up being the real thing.

When the midnight watch changed on what was supposed to be Monday, May 21, 1945, we were informed that we were to skip that day and assume that it was Tuesday, May 22. I did a little research and learned that the Navy divided the earth's surface into 24 time zones, each bounded by meridians of 15 degrees, or one hour apart in longitude.

Greenwich, England, has the distinct honor of being the location where all of this official stuff starts. We were navigating in the west longitude and made our changes of time under the rule of plus zones. We had just crossed over the International Date Line. Talk aboard ship at this juncture mostly hinged around the many wagers of when we would gain back those two extra days when we returned to the states.

**Ensign Weber, taking his turn on the "conn"**

# SHROUT - AFTER the MUD

Wednesday, May 23, saw the entire ship assume condition two. We had been having regular soundings of general quarters and knew that water activity about us had picked up. More and more aircraft were being spotted-- friendly planes, to our welcomed relief. We spent the entire night on condition two. I spelled Hager, our radar man, on watching the PPI scope. It was comforting to know that radar could see through the dark of night and alert us to possible targets several miles distant. When we were under condition one, I found it very spooky standing watch in the forward gun tub, gazing out into the dark night. I had no way of knowing just what was out there. My time in the radio shack standing radar watch helped sooth my concerns.

After several nights of standing watch in our gun tub, I came upon the bright idea that I could help pass the time by doing some of my impressions. I would say, "Listen up guys, who do you think this is?" I would go into my best northeastern accent and say, "My friends, Fala hates war, Eleanor hates war, and I hate war and Eleanor." I would get chuckles out of the guys. The guys really must have been bored, for they would request me to do my imitations time after time. I could also do a pretty good James Cagney.

On the morning of Thursday, May 24, 1945, while standing in the morning chow line, I could tell that we were slowing our speed. General quarters was sounded. We dropped our food trays anyplace we could get them to stay put and headed to our stations-- on the double.

The sea was normal and the sun had been up for a while. We could clearly see the horizon. I did not see any ships or see any planes in the sky, but I did see what looked like land off the starboard beam. Sure enough, there it was, a small island of the Marshall Island group. We learned later it was called Mejit Island. I estimated the distance to the island to be about three miles. It had been rumored that the Japanese were lurking in this area, and our skipper wanted to be sure we would be ready. We secured from general quarters an hour later, and went back to finish our morning chow that had become cold by this time. The duty cook recognized this situation and made a new batch for us to devour. Sea air really enhanced one's appetite.

Thursday and Friday found us slowly zig - zagging through the islands with speeds being reduced from time to time. It seemed to me that we were spending most of our time either in condition two or at our general quarters stations. I was getting used to running to my side of the 40 mm, tossing the cover aside, and each time fully expecting to start pushing clips of 40 mm ammo into the magazine. We did not load until told to do so. It was quite a project to remove the unspent rounds of ammo.

211

## SHROUT - AFTER the MUD

As I stood in the Saturday six o'clock breakfast chow line, I watched our progress through the many atolls of the Marshalls. The sea was calm and there did not appear to be anything in this part of the world that could motivate any fear within us. Everything looked serene and peaceful. I could not detect  the degree of high emotion that was prevalent in all of the crew's minds and thoughts earlier in the week.

As I progressed along the narrow deck walkway towards the hatch just outside the galley, I found myself thinking how misleading this could be to one's real inner thoughts.  We were supposed to be at war and fast approaching that part of the world where nations were shooting at one another.  At the same time, I was wondering what nice surprise would be awaiting me for breakfast.  It was so easy to be lulled into a state of unreadiness.

The Marshall Islands looked peaceful.  I did not see any indication that the Japanese had been here.  We were told that we had destroyed or scared them away.  The Americans did not attempt to occupy all of the islands because there were so many.  Some of the rumors were that the enemy might still be hiding in the tiny jungle covered atolls. The thought that they still could be lurking someplace made most of us extremely nervous.

My day dreaming was abruptly interrupted, as well as the breakfast I had started to eat. Loud and clear came the all too familiar sound of general quarters. I was beginning to wonder just how many times we could keep rushing to our battle stations and maintain a spirit and attitude of true readiness. Quickly these thoughts dissipated from my thinking. I knew that I was in the middle of war and must concentrate on my assignment as the first loader of my assigned weapon of war.

General quarters proved to be another time to be ready, just in case. With general quarters secured, breakfast was finished. As we watched from the deck rail in very normal weather and a calm sea, we noticed that we were entering a large harbor. Rumors drifted about the ship that we were about to drop anchor in Eniwetok Harbor. This we accomplished at 1007. We were anchored just off the *AKA-41.* In fact our first anchoring had to be changed. We were much too close and did not stand off far enough to suit the Skipper.

During the next couple days, I noticed there were no alerts at anytime. We spent those two days moving from one supply source to another. I noted that we could not do all these tasks one right after the other. We always had to return to our anchoring positioning, let the anchor out, wait awhile, pull up anchor, and go get the next item. I suppose it kept us occupied and out of trouble.

There was a tall, black sailor named Himes, who was assigned to cater to the commissioned officers. The Navy called those who did this type of work, stewards. They served the meals to the officers in their special state room; they laundered and pressed their uniforms. I wondered what this must be like to be waited upon. Must have been nice. Our ship's steward was from Louisiana. Man, he was strong looking and liked to show any of us that asked just how strong he really was.

My early life on the Indiana farm very seldom provided an opportunity for me to observe any cultural differences in those of a different race. My mother consistently made me aware that people were just people.

During my years in the Akron Public Schools and living in the small rural community, I never witnessed any strong racial resentment, one way or the other. Once every year or so, I might have the opportunity to drive through the streets of Peru, a larger community about thirty miles south of Akron. On a few of these rare occasions, I might have seen a black man or woman on the streets as we passed, but I never thought anything about it. A black lady attended my church and I would see her occasionally. Her husband worked for the local sawmill. I never had reason to doubt my mother's teaching. In the innocence of singing in Sunday School and Bible School

214

about Jesus loving   the little children of the world, whatever the color,  I accepted my shipmates equally.

Himes and I became very good friends and we spent many hours in various types of conversations.  He loved to talk about Bible scriptures.   Himes had difficulty in reading, and  I could soon tell he needed some help.  I read to him from the Bible, and he let me know that he appreciated it.  He talked to me about his wife and how much he loved her, but couldn't seem  to put it into writing just how he really felt.  "Willie, (that's what I called him) how would you like for me to write to her for you, I asked?"

Stenciled on one of my white caps was C. Shrout. For some reason the W.C. that should have been there did not make it.  This occasion was another of the times that he seemed to enjoy addressing  me by using my cap name. "I sure would like for you do just that,  C. Stroud," Willie would say in his heavy voice.  Shrout became Stroud to Willie.   I would usually do the letter writing for Willie during the daytime when we had time to ourselves.  Many times we would choose a secluded spot on the fantail of the ship.  This would provide the privacy he needed to tell me what he wanted to relay to his wife.  He would sign the letters and would tell me every time that I sure could write good.  "Stroud, you know just what to say," Willie would tell me.

Tuesday, May 29, we received our new orders to leave Eniwetok Atoll. It seemed that every time we pulled up anchor to leave any port or island that might be close by, we would have a call to general quarters to check for unauthorized absentees. I couldn't imagine anyone wanting to be left behind on some desolate island. But, I guess Navy procedure wanted to make sure. With all of this paper work behind us, we headed out to sea. We set our heading to 277T. As we left the sight of land, our activity of rushing to our battle stations again resumed. General quarters was sounded every couple hours the rest of that day. Sometimes we would see ships on the horizon. The first day out, we saw nine ships in a group. They turned out to be our own *LSTs*. I noticed, that the group of ships we were a part of this time was much larger than before.

We were told we were part of a large convoy and we could tell that we were heading in a southwestwardly direction. Ships had been collecting at Eniwetok, and we joined them to give perimeter protection. We had only to guess where we were going next. I had done considerable map study before leaving the states and was pretty sure we were headed towards the Caroline Islands.

Wednesday morning at 0530, we were awakened with "General quarters, man your battle stations, hurry men, this is it!" We all rushed to our stations totally expecting to see enemy gun barrels pointed at us. Two

216

large spheres had loomed in the water in front of us and were dodged by some quick maneuvering. The *LCS 72* and *LCS 4* left formation and chased the spheres down and sank them. I could hear the 40 mms loud peeling sounds and the ear splitting sounds of the mines bursting, as the two ships accomplished their assigned task. This activity was to be a quick reminder of what the coming sounds of war would most likely resemble. The two ships that did the mine disposal assignment quickly rejoined our formation, and we continued on into the early morning.

So this is what it would be like, I was thinking to myself; so quick, so fast, and it could all be over. All of this caused me to meditate considerably about why we were here and what might be ahead just over the horizon. Our hours on watch duty took on a new determination. We all had registered just how easy it would be to plow into a floating mine. Each man decided to be more vigilant and to take gun watch more seriously that he had before.

Friday, June 1, found us setting our clocks and watches back another hour to conform to minus 10 zone time. We moved ahead a full day, ten days ago, and now we were reversing the procedure an hour at a time. I suppose if we were to go all the way around the world we would eventually add all of the gained time back on our clocks. Never in my wildest dreams while living on the farm, would I have thought that this would be an issue in my life.  Many of the farmers fussed about daylight saving time.  That was just moving it forward  one hour in the spring and then back one hour in the fall.  In a matter of a few days, I found myself winding the hands on my wrist watch back and forth many times.    The world was changing about me, and I was finding that I had to conform in order to exist within it.

A new game was introduced to some of us.  The city boys talked us into playing "flinch" with them.  Much of the time in the south seas we wore only white skivie shirts, or sometimes we could get by with no shirt at all.  Our tanned muscular bare arms became easy targets for a shipmate's punch with his bare fist.  One punch was free.  If you as much as showed a slight bit of flinching, the one delivering the punch to your arm had ten more free swats at your bare upper arm.  If he elected to take the gifted swipes at what was  now becoming your slightly sore arm, he had to allow you to test his arm in similar fashion.  This would be repeated over and over again, until someone elected not to take advantage of his golden opportunity to pulverize his shipmate's arm. What fun, the instigators thought!   I did not like to nurse a swollen arm that ached for hours at a time.  I did not initiate any contests, but had to be a part of many challenges that were thrust my way.

Saturday, we had gunnery practice by shooting at AA (anti-aircraft) balloons launched by *LCS 103*.  We needed to keep our minds sharp on our battle station assignments, and this was a good method to employ. Even with ear plugs, firing 40 mms. in rapid fire is deafening. I can still hear the sounds, decades later. About an hour after we had secured from gunnery practice, general quarters was sounded. I wondered if we had alerted the Japanese of our presence in the area, with all of the noise we made. We went into a zig - zag maneuver with our column of ships. We went one direction for a couple minutes and then changed course.

Every day we were called to our battle stations. There were no exceptions. Some days we went to alert three and four times a day. We were in the real war zone now. The Japanese could be anywhere. They could be off the horizon in ships or below the surface in subs. We had to be alert and ready for anything. Some evenings we did not get much sleep. It seems we were up and down to respond to general quarters several times a night.

Monday, June 4, saw the convoy entering Mugai Channel, and into the Ulithi Islands. We were now in the Western Carolines. There was not a lot of talk or news about the Ulithi Atolls and the part they played in the war for the United States. They were an excellent spot for the Americans to collect many of its battle weary small boats and have them repaired.

219

Upon entering the harbor, I was really surprised at what my eyes saw! Something of great importance must be about ready to happen. There were ships of all kinds as far as the eye could see. The Ulithi Atolls made an excellent safe harbor from the rough seas. We first moored portside to *LCS 72.* Then, after dark we moved away out in the channel and dropped our own anchor off one of the Ulithi Islands.

Early Tuesday we were pleasantly surprised with the mail launch coming along side. I had not received any mail since Pearl Harbor. This mail call produced thirty-one letters for me. I sorted them by sender and then chronologically by date. What fun to read of home and those that cared for me and were pulling for me. I wrote my letters to friends and family in the states each evening. I would drop them in the mail box slot just as if they were going to be mailed the next day. When we were out to sea, mailing of the letters could be deferred for many days.

All of the enlisted men's mail had to be censured or read to make sure it did not contain anything that might threaten our ship's safety. Ensign Paul Weber was our communications officer, and this task fell into his list of responsibilities. He must have become very bored reading our outgoing mail. I'm sure he solicited some of the other officers to assist him. After all, they needed a laugh or two. Some of the outgoing mail must have been hilarious.

A type of mail we used was called "V-mail." It had to be written on special paper and then transferred to film and flown to the mainland. The film was developed and enlarged, then printed and sent on to the addressee. Before leaving the states I had designed a special code with my brother, Irvin, for letting him know in what part of the world I was at any given time. I would use the first letter of each word of the first words of my letter to spell out the location. It worked! A lot of my mail was chopped with holes or deleted, but never were the code locations tampered with. Some of the beginning sentences must have sounded very strange. Sometimes It would take me a long time to say what I wanted to express and still make sense.

Wednesday, Thursday, and Friday were spent taking on supplies, fuel, ammo, and water. It sure took a lot of supplies to run a ship, even as small as ours. The Captain said the meat we were eating was getting freezer burned and ordered the entire meat locker dumped overboard. The sharks and other meat eating creatures of the sea sure had a feast that day, at the expense of the American taxpayer.

The weekend was uneventful and sort of relaxing. It made me wonder if we were possibly heading for something big? We wrote a lot of letters and small talked among ourselves a great deal about home and our loved ones. We did not have any general quarters while in the Ulithi Island immediate area. I have thought a lot about that since. Here was gathered perhaps the largest armada of American shipping. Hundreds, perhaps thousands of all sizes and useful purposes, and yet the Japanese left us alone. Perhaps we had managed to push the Japs further back towards their homeland, and they had no way to know of our existence.

Tuesday, June 12, we had orders to join another convoy that was already in the formation made in and about the Ulithi group. We pulled up anchor and left the Mugai Channel and took our position on the perimeter of the convoy. There was a reason we positioned ourselves there. We were much smaller and had less men to loose, if hit by enemy fire. We were the decoys, so to speak. We could make a smoke screen, if needed, with a couple fog generators that were located on the fantail. In a dense screen of fog it was very difficult for the enemy to do any effective bombing or shelling

What a sea of ships to gaze upon! I noted that the vastness of it stretched as far as the eye could see to our port side. We were on the outer starboard perimeter of the huge convoy. I knew that I was a part, small though it might be, of a major development soon to take place in the Pacific.

**The Skipper, (Lt. Carlton) and Ensign Storm (with cap) keeping a careful watch on what was ahead of the 73**

Wednesday, June 13, our convoy moved ahead in the easterly part of the Philippine Sea in a northwesterly direction. I thought that we must be heading for Japan itself. This particular convoy moved at a much slower speed a lot of the time, moving forward at only seven knots. All of the large cargo ships were heavily loaded and moved very slow. Our job was to protect them, so we had to stay close by. I knew that all of the large cargo ships were carrying supplies and ammunition to the front line.

I thought at times that I was like an old mother hen protecting her chicks back on the farm in Indiana. Only this "old mother hen" was so much smaller than her chicks. I started to wonder just what it would be like to take a hit from a Japanese plane. It could be a small bomb or perhaps an aerial torpedo. I decided to take each day, one at a time. I was at war, and war was not defined as anything pleasant.

# 7.

# OKINAWA

## The Front at Last

The next five days saw an usual amount of alerts to general quarters and the occasional making of smoke. Early Monday morning, June 18, we saw by first light of day our initial look at the islands of Okinawa. The Americans had invaded Okinawa on April 1 and were in need of supplies. We had been part of a large convoy and had brought those needed supplies with us. I had early watch that morning and, while yet dark, could see gunfire on the shore. We were summoned to general quarters at 0734 and remained at our stations for three hours before securing.

During all of this time, we were maneuvering in and about the channels and small harbors and were ready to start shooting, if called upon. Shortly before noon we had dropped anchor off Hagushi, Okinawa. I learned later that

225

while I was watching the gunfire on the beach, General Simon Buckner was killed by a shell blast as he observed the Marines moving through the brush to an ultimate victory. History proved that General Buckner was the highest ranking American officer to be killed during all of World War ll. The Japanese were not shooting out across the water at us. I was in a much safer position than the General had been.

After evening chow was completed, we pulled anchor and started the first of many after dusk anti-aircraft patrols. The radar scope was the instrument used to measure the distance to the shoreline in the dark. The ever changing shoreline made its outline on the scope. We could put our range bug or marker on the edge and could be fairly accurate as to where the shore line was. The skipper always allowed for reefs and such, and we managed to stay out of trouble. Watching the scope was a fascinating assignment, and I felt very important in performing it.

I stood my share of the radar watches all through the night. It was a difficult assignment which became very tiring to my eyes, just to keep watching the sweeping arch of light go round and round the circular PPI scope. But I also realized that my assignment in front of the scope was very necessary to keep us off the rocks and reefs. I dared not look away or let my mind wander. We could not see land in the dark. The Japanese were realizing their predicament and some were swimming away from what they felt was certain death. The water might be their end, but some thought it worth a chance and did try it. We had men posted with rifles on the bow and the stern ready to shoot any they saw.

Our first night of patrol was uneventful. I really was glad. It could have been much more threatening to us than a man swimming in the water. There could have been mines. We were told to be extra cautious of anything in the water that could look like a tree log that might appear to be just floating along. Some could be small suicide boats or rafts loaded with explosives ready to be pushed into the sides of our ships and then detonate.

As I attempted to get some sleep the first evening in enemy territory, I kept thinking of my mother's kitchen and what she might be fixing for breakfast on that day. I was only about 360 miles from Japan. When I thought of this and considered just how far it was to my Indiana farm home, I was devastated. The time difference made this a realistic feeling. I was experiencing my first night of impending combat about a half-mile from the enemy. I had already watched men, ours and theirs, crawling about in the brush on shore. The Marines were shooting star shells that would burst and illuminate the area, making it almost as bright as day. I could see the silhouettes as they crawled about in the thick brush. This was it! Harms way was just a short distance off our starboard bow.

I had flashbacks of watching early war movies at the Madrid Theater back in Akron, and here I was watching the war "live." However, I felt very secure at the time. I did not think that any danger would harm our ship or me. When there are no guns trained upon you, a relaxed attitude can engulf your being.

Here I was, munching on an apple, starting to find myself entertained by the enemy and our American Marines as they sparred at one another in the brush just a few yards away. I told myself, "This is not real, I can not be seeing what I think I am." But it was true. My mind drifted back to the old cow barn on the Shewman farm. There, on earlier occasions, I would sit on a three-legged stool milking away on, Bess, the cow. At the same time, I was wondering what it must be like at the battle front. Now I was there! Just a few yards away from where all hell was breaking loose.

When I slowly returned to my place of rest in hole number one, I told myself that I must get used to this. They were not just playing games out there a few yards from where I was to lay my head for the evening. Men would be trying to kill one another. Pleasant dreams, I thought, as I tried to keep my eyes closed and go to sleep.

However, Tuesday morning, June 19, 1945 did arrive. As I banged my breakfast chow tray in the GI can, I found it difficult to look across at the close shoreline and think of what was happening there. I had slept so peacefully all night. It was hard to think that men who had never seen one another before were eliminating each other. I could hear gun-fire as I cleaned up my shiny tray from which I had just enjoyed a good meal. Unbelievable was the word! Will all of this unnecessary killing ever stop? I forced myself to dismiss the pangs of guilt in being a part of such a destructive intent. The idea of destroying something or somebody dominated my current thoughts.

All of my early training at home and school had reasoned with me, and convinced me life was precious and one must help preserve it at all costs. Yet, here I was, part of an intended destructive force that flew in the face of my early teachings. I suppose others of my shipmates were going through the same emotional agonizing. We were all very private on such matters; I never knew for sure what they were really thinking.

We left our overnight anchorage and moored starboard to USS LST #134 and received 200 Mark VII hand mines. We were to have the mines available if we saw the enemy swimming in the water. The fact that we could see and hear activity on the shore made the need for more weaponry realistic.

The hand mine was about the size of a thick book and had a bail-type handle.  The hand mine was secured with a safety pin, similar to what  a hand grenade had. Our instructions were upon seeing the enemy in the water, to pull the pin and  heave it as far as we could.  The concussion created in the water from its discharge  was enough to kill the swimmer.  There was so much noise from shore activity that it made little consequence when we practiced tossing  the mines.  This was our first chance to experiment with them.  It was a little scary.  I kept wondering if I would ever freeze and hold onto the handle and not throw it.

As I watched the daylight disappear and the shadows of night develop, I really had very little to do. With the possibility of general quarters being announced at any moment, we did not attempt to do any deck work.  I thought to myself that I probably would never have a situation quite like this again.  We did have to eat, and some things must go on.  Mess cooks could be observed sitting on the main deck, peeling potatoes for our next meal and watching the sky but not seeing anything.  All of us on deck were listening and watching the big battleships lob huge sixteen inch shells into the island.

I remember thinking to myself, "Could something like this be possible?"  The battleships were out of sight, but we could hear the deep heavy sounds of detonation and then the whizzing sound of the projectile as it moved overhead, bound for its intended point of destruction. What a scary time it must have been for the enemy holed up in some cave on the island. I could not imagine what it must have been like to be close to where those sixteen inch projectiles hit. In our training, we were told that when a battleship fired a sixteen-inch gun it was like shooting an object the weight of a small car, twenty-six miles with extreme accuracy.

Later in the day, about 1300, we weighed anchor and raced to a position several yards off our port beam. A Naval Hellcat fighter had crashed in the water. The Skipper was on the conn and ordered the engine room to go to flank speed. Word passed swiftly among the crew about the kind of mission we were on. Besides that, we had heard that if and when we rescued a downed pilot, the carrier he was assigned to would furnish ice cream to the rescuing ship. I had not tasted ice cream in weeks!

We arrived on the scene very quickly and discovered our sister ship, the 72, had made the water extraction of the pilot and were already anticipating their reward. I did not wish any bad luck towards any of our American flyers. To the contrary, I wanted them to be as successful as possible. But I remembered how good homemade ice cream tasted when we made it back home. I thought it sure would go down good about now.

**The twin 40 mm located in front of the conn
The author's general quarters station
was to the right of the twin barrels**

That evening we anchored off a large merchant ship discharging cargo. This was probably one of the large cargo ships we had escorted to Okinawa. Tonight we were acting as a screen. We received an alert at 2206 via radio to make smoke, condition red, control green. We made smoke for about fifteen minutes and condition white was flashed by radio. This meant we could secure from general quarters.

Standing in the dark of night on my 40 mm gun mount was becoming a common occurrence. Many hours were spent just waiting for the unknown. Eventually, I learned to pass time with small talk with my other shipmates in our gun tub. We talked about things back home, speculating on just how long this war would last.

General quarters was again sounded at 0215. I ran as fast as I could, climbing the ladder out of our sleeping hole, two rungs at a time. On deck it was as dark as pitch. I could not see a thing. The atmospheric conditions had caused the fog we had made earlier to still linger in the area. I knew we were anchored very close to other ships, from what I had remembered in the daylight hours. I could just imagine that one of the large destroyers closest to us would forget we were there and swing their guns our direction and I might be looking right down one of the gun barrels. I was relieved to see when the fog began to lift that the destroyer guns were pointed away from our ship.

We finally secured from the early morning general quarters and I got a little shut eye. I found that I was getting used to this up and down routine--a short snooze and back again to my battle station.

Later that morning, the Skipper had three of us lower the Captain's gig into the water. After we had the gig in the water we were told to row over to the battleship *Tennessee* where they would give us some ice cream. We were really excited at this order and started the short journey across the span of water between the *Tennessee* and the **73.** I noticed the closer we came to the big battleship, the smaller we looked in comparison, and the smaller I felt about the whole thing.

Little and Spencer were on the oars and started having trouble steering our small boat to the *Tennessee's* gangway ladder that was extended down the side of the ship. The more they tried to get it lined up with the ladder, the more we would go around and around. Finally, the officer on duty at the top of the *Tennessee* gangway used his bullhorn and announced, "Ahoy in the small boat, perhaps you should just stand by and we will pull up anchor and come by you." What a downer that was! I had been along as the extra man to give Little and Spencer support. I felt like I was six inches tall.

Finally after another couple attempts, the guys managed to get our small boat to come alongside the gangway, and we received our supply of ice cream. No one said anything about our difficulty in maneuvering the gig to our shipmates when we returned to the **73**. We really did not have to say anything--all aboard were only interested in devouring the ice cream.


# Okinawa Secured


Fighting on Okinawa ceased on June 21, 1945. The Japanese had enough. We did not hear of the news on-board the **73** for several days. We knew something had happened, because we were not doing dusk patrol any more. However, this did not deter the Kamikaze planes from keeping us up all night. We could count on at least two awakings to general quarters each evening. We would stand in our battle stations without having the fire power to reach the planes and watch the big guns of the battleships and cruisers shoot them out of the sky. On some occasions, the American shore batteries were able to destroy the suicide planes.

From my battle station I watched the search lights play all over the sky trying to find the Kamikaze. As the searchlights crossed upon the tiny object bearing destruction for me and my shipmates, I watched the shore batteries send their screaming shells skyward. I knew all too well that the intent was to totally destroy the aircraft and its occupant.

I could not help from thinking about my earlier days and how my mother and my Sunday school teachers had taught me to love everyone, no matter what their color. Now I found myself in a hopeful mood wanting the shells to make direct contact with the enemy. I had to quickly sort the former days of instruction from the reality of the now. At that moment, that is exactly what the Kamikaze were-- "yellow" though they may be--they were my enemy.

During a daylight raid, one of the Kamikaze planes, after being hit by American gunfire, crashed close to our ship. We heard later that the pilot was dead. When another ship closer by fished his body out of the water, they reported to the rest of us that he was wearing a black uniform. This seemed a little eerie to me. The Japanese were really getting desperate in attacking us singularly and in broad daylight. I hoped this would soon end.

Midnight of the day the Japanese surrendered the island of Okinawa to the Americans, we were making smoke as usual with instructions to screen the immediate area against low flying suicide planes. Something happened to the smoke generator apparatus and it caught fire.  Excitement broke out on the fantail of the **73**. Standing where I was  on my 40 mm  gun mount, I could not see through the deck house, but I could sure hear the commotion.  One of my shipmates, Klakulak, received second degree burns  on his arms, hands, face, and ears. Our ship's pharmacist's mate, Moyer, and a Navy doctor, Lt. Hoffman, who happened to be on aboard that day, gave Klakulak emergency treatment.  He looked pretty bad to me when I saw him.  Later that day they transferred Klakulak to the hospital ship *USS Samaritan* for more extensive treatment.

Wednesday, June 27, 1945, had been an uneventful day.  There were no daytime battle station orders.  But nighttime proved to be different.  A couple hours before dark, we pulled up anchor and moved closer to a nesting of larger ships to offer smoke protection.  Two hours after dark, general quarters was again sounded.  I hurriedly took my position and searched the horizon.  Sure enough, a Kamikaze pilot had found his way past us and had hit the carrier *Bunker Hill*.  I could not see through all of the fog we and others like us were making, but we heard the explosion and were told later what had happened.

There were many causalities on-board the carrier. One Japanese flyer and a plane load of destruction changed the lives of many American families in just a few minutes that evening.  I had thought the war just might be slowing down.  I was not quite correct.  To those families who lost loved ones that night, the war in their world had not diminished, only intensified.

## The Kamikaze Would Not Quit

On and on the suicide planes came at us.  Some nights it seemed like we were forever at our battle stations. Many of us became very weary from lack of sleep.  I am one of those people that can not fall asleep at the drop of a hat.  This resulted in a horrible image being  vividly implanted in my mind, as I  moved between my station in general quarters and my pillow in hole number one.  It was very difficult to dismiss the scene of watching human life explode into eternity, high in the skies over Okinawa. Somehow, all of this did not seem right.  On the nights we were repeatedly  summoned to our gun mounts, the deeply embedded thoughts of observing death would not  leave my weary mind.  Eventually after  putting my head gently to my pillow, I found  much solace in letting my thoughts wander back to my days and nights growing up on the Indiana farm.

We adopted a new name for our evening patrol assignments.  We started calling it "flycatcher" time.  This expression reminded me of the fly ribbons we would hang up to catch flies on the farm.    There must have been a terrible rumor out amongst the enemy that to be caught by the Americans was a miserable fate. Consequently, more and more Japanese were killed swimming away from land.

Talk among the crew was of a new name given to our location. "Nakgusuku Wan" had been changed to "Buckner Bay" in honor of General Buckner. The General was killed while observing troop action the first night we arrived at Okinawa.

I will always remember July 6, 1945. Early in the evening in broad daylight, a Kamikaze plane with guns blazing attempted to strafe the **73,** only to have his bursts of fire ripple the water on each side  of the ship.  No hits were made, probably because we were so small compared to other ships. An LCS  only had a 23 foot beam.

The strafing happened  during chow time when most of the crew were below deck.  The duty signalman was the only witness to this near disaster.  With all of the rockets, hand mines, 40 mm and 20 mm ammo that we carried, we would have been like a powder keg.

Three weeks later I would learn that on this very same day of my near demise,  my mother died.  Because of the usual  delays in receiving mail, my first news was a hastily written letter from my sister, Verna, that Mother was very sick. After reading this disturbing news from my sister, I quickly checked the remaining mail for more news from her. Sure enough, there was another letter from my sister and it was postmarked a couple days later than the first. I was afraid to open it. But I did--and there was the dreaded news. My shipmates were very supportive and the skipper called me to his stateroom and gave me his condolences in person.

It did not seem to matter how often the suicide planes came over; we were constantly involved in many odd jobs about the ship. I began to wonder if Boats (Onufer) had x-ray vision. I would be told to use a chipping hammer and chip what looked like perfectly good paint from the deck. Some places I just knew I had applied new paint only days before. The reason we were told this had to be done was to prevent rust from getting any kind of toe-hold on the steel decks. This was the seaman's lot in Naval life, to do what seemed like mundane chores and odd jobs. I really did not object too much. I wanted the war to end and I wanted to go home. The deck repair assignments and other trifle duties helped pass the time. It was during some of these hours that I became better acquainted with shipmates. Stress level was minimal when working on the deck compared to when we really got cranked up during battle station's.

"Ship's service" was the retail store for our ship. Its location started out in the mess hall. Stockwell, a radioman by rating, was in charge. He kept candy, gum, cigarettes, stationery, pens, pencils, soaps, and a few other sundries available for the crew to purchase. Later, the Captain decided we needed a better place to do our shopping. We pulled up anchor, left the area and went a short distance out to sea. An ammo storage locker was relieved of its inventory. We gave many rounds of 40 mm the "deep six," and simply tossed it overboard into the ocean and returned to our original anchorage.

The storage locker was large enough for Stockwell to stand inside and work his merchandise. All he had to do when he wanted to close, was to batten the cover. I do not believe this action would have had the Navy's approval. We had a good Skipper who was constantly thinking of his men and their welfare.

The month of July moved very slowly. It seemed to me from what small amount of news we were privy to, that the energy the world was expending to further the activities of war, was moving at a much slower pace. I learned later that America was experimenting with a new device of destruction, first labeled, "Trinity," and then dubbed, "Fat Man."

On July 15 this new instrument of havoc was detonated over Alamogordo, New Mexico. Not many Americans realized on the eve of that eventful day, how this event would eventually change the course of World War II and ultimately the path and destiny of life as man knew it. The atomic age had arrived in fatal fashion.

A couple days after the Alamogordo incident, we rushed to general quarters at early dusk. The Kamikaze were getting wiser and were making their attack approaches just as the sun was starting to set. If they positioned themselves between their target and the sun it made it very difficult to see them as they approached. The suicide pilot knew to stay just over the water. This evening there were two planes that attacked. Both missed the intended targets and crashed into the sea. From my position standing on the gun turret, I could not see any activity in the water. We learned after securing from our stations what had happened. Japan had lost two more Kamikaze pilots.

Early Sunday morning, July 22, 1945, general quarters was sounded at 0214. From my gun mount I could hear the anchor winches humming, meaning we were pulling anchor for some reason. The air was heavy with smoke that other support ships had started to make. Our assignment was to get moving as soon as we could and to render aid to the *USS APA200*. She had received an aerial

242

torpedo in the port bow. Another Kamikaze had made it through the perimeter of small support ships like ours and succeeded in a direct hit. We spent the rest of the night laying to, ready to lend assistance. Twenty men came aboard for morning chow from the damaged *APA*. It seemed that they were making their own temporary repairs, but the galley was out of commission.

I was glad to see daylight. It was kind of spooky standing next to my 40 mm gun, peering out into the darkness, and not knowing for sure what was going to happen next. The stench of gunpowder from the detonated torpedo attempted to mingle with the oily smell of fog made from recently operated fog generators. The combination of all this did not create a pleasant aroma. Any thoughts that I might have had about how good morning chow might be quickly left.

July disappeared into history, but as it made its slow journey it managed to record daily, time after time, the tiresome event of our rushing to battle stations. I was introduced to the new month of August with an announcement that a typhoon was brewing. The **73** and its crew bobbed up and down and managed to weather the high winds that came along with the warning. I, along with the rest of the deck crew, kept busy checking lines making sure all were battened down tightly. We secured from the storm and began our usual exercise of ponderment of what the next few days would bring.    My mind went back to home and the Indiana farm.  I remember thinking August 3 was my oldest sister's birthday and that several of my family must be making homemade ice cream to help celebrate the event.  I loved those family occasions and felt terrible that I was missing out on this fun time.  Besides that, I loved homemade ice cream!

## Hiroshima and the Atomic Bomb

Not one of our crew  had any idea what catastrophic news the month of August was about to deliver to the world.   I learned later that negotiations were being attempted with Japanese during this time, but Japan was formally rejecting the surrender ultimatum.

At precisely 0915, August 6, 1945, the **73** and its crew were anchored safely in Buckner Bay, Okinawa Shima.  I was occupied with pleasant thoughts of what a great meal Carriger, ship's cook, had presented to the crew that morning.  Rumor had it we were to pull up anchor and move closer to the mail ship.  Great, this meant another mail call! I dearly loved to receive mail from back home.

Looking back now, it is very difficult to imagine what it must have been like at that precise moment in Hiroshima, Japan, some 400 miles off our starboard bow.

244

History tells us that at that moment in Japan's history, "Little Boy" was unleashed upon them and the entire city of Hiroshima, Japan, was destroyed. It was said "only one blackened tree remained." Atomic bomb number one had been delivered to Japan by President Truman's command.

While Emperor Hirohita assessed the damage of this single bomb drop, another atomic bomb, "Fat Man" was detonated over the city of Nagasaki, Japan, on August 9. This turned out to be the final blow needed to end the war.

To the crew of the **73** and others anchored in Buckner Bay, knowledge of the war about to end was not known. In fact, we continued to have Kamikaze raids. We went about the business of war in our usual way. In the evenings we moved the ship from one vantage point to another, depending upon which way the wind was blowing. We used the wind to help us screen the larger ships that were assigned to us. This was the old mother hen and chicks comparison.

***USS Pennsylvania, BB38***
**A battleship the 73 was assigned to cover with a
smoke screen on the night of August 12, 1945**

246

After evening chow on August 12, 1945, the Skipper decided to move the **73,** just in case we were called upon to screen the large battleship off our port bow. At 2045 we heard a loud scraping sound coming from under our hull. The **73** moved ever so slightly and the lights we had on below deck went out.  We quickly solved the problem and restored the lights.

Not much was said at that time about what had happened.  We did go to general quarters when the lights went out and the fog generators started making smoke.  All was quiet during the time of standing ready at our battle stations.  I could feel a strangeness in the air.  Something had happened, but we were not told anything.  I guess no news was available.  The **73** secured from general quarters and back to the sack I went.  Dreamland arrived, and I was oblivious to what   life was dealing with just a few yards off our port bow.  I was in my own little world, and at that moment all was safe and sound around me and my shipmates.

Early the next morning upon arriving on deck, I could see what had happened.  There  had been a surprise attack by the Kamikaze.  A plane with  an aerial fish  had made a successful run.  The Kamikaze had slipped by before we could make smoke.   The aerial torpedo had been set to run a little shallow and it actually scraped our hull, shorting out the electrical system!  The torpedo then continued on, hitting the *USS Pennsylvania*, the battleship we had been assigned to screen. As I looked off our port side I could easily see the *Pennsylvania* listing to starboard.

The "something is wrong" feeling I had during general quarters last night had some authenticity. Nineteen dead American men and ten of their wounded shipmates were being gathered from the damaged area of the *Pennsylvania*. Something within me had given me this strange feeling. It was difficult to eat morning chow with the paleness of the hour looming just off our port side.

Earlier in July, I had the opportunity to visit a friend aboard a destroyer. His name was Joe Wildermuth, and he was from my home town of Akron, Indiana. His ship was also anchored in Buckner Bay. He was an officer and arranged to bring his ship's gig by the **73** and pick me up. I had the privilege on a Sunday while in Buckner Bay to go to chapel with him and have noon chow in the officers' mess on his ship. I really felt important.

My friend, Joe, upon looking around for my ship, on the morning of August 13, 1945, noticed we had disappeared from the bay area. He knew the Kamikaze had made hits the night before and assumed the **73** had gone down defending the *Pennsylvania*. In his correspondence to his family and friends, he mentioned

248

what he thought had happened. I later found out that for several days, people around my hometown were hesitant to mention this sort of news to my dad, not knowing if he had heard any news about me. Finally, a neighbor caught my dad on one of his downtown Akron shopping trips and mentioned the incident to him. Dad said to him, "Oh no, we just heard from Bill and we believe he is in the Phillipines." Apparently my coding system was working in my communications back home to the family. The **73** had received orders to leave for the Phillipines early the morning after the attack on the *Pennsylvania.* It was a natural assumption that my ship could have been destroyed. If the torpedo had been riding just an inch or so higher I would not be writing this chronicle!

**The *USS Pennsylvania*, getting assistance the next day
Visit web site http://www.USSPENNSYLVANIA.com
for more information regarding this great ship**

## The Phillipines and War No More

August 13, 1945, we secured anchor at 0856 and started moving out of the channel into the harbor passing through the harbor net gates. Shortly after noon chow, we assumed our position in a convoy and headed in a southerly direction. Now where were we going?

Four days later, and without any general quarters being sounded, I saw land off our starboard bow. I viewed the land sighting from my vantage point on deck. I had ventured topside after finishing morning chow. Later, I found out the land was the southern tip of Samar, one of the Phillipine Islands. We made our way into the San Pedro Bay, Leyte, and moored along the starboard side of the *LCS 70*. Our first night was spent in another one of those strange, distant sounding lands that I had read about in school while studying the countries of the world. Akron, Indiana, at this moment, seemed so far away.

## Leyte's Beach, Ball, Beer and Bum Boats

The war was coming to a finish. This time in the history of World War ll, negotiations were in the beginning process to officially accept Japan's surrender. In fact, while we were at Samar, not far away in Manila, American officials were discussing the arrangements with Japanese heads of state.

Our duty time was limited. We did not do many deck maintenance assignments. Instead, we were to be on official R&R (rest and recreation).

The second day at Samar, we pulled up anchor and moved the **73** deeper into the island group. I could not see any cities, only jungle-like growth I had seen in movies. We stopped close to an island that had a sandy beach. Captain Carlton was on the conn and he ordered the two stern anchors to be away. With anchors down, the **73** headed for shore, letting out anchor cable as we went. Our ship with its flat bottom slid upon the smooth sand and listed slightly to the port. It seemed all of the crew knew exactly what to do. Over the port side we scampered. We had to wade ashore, but who cared, we were on land! There was fun ahead and we would get the opportunity to stretch our ship-weary legs.

252

The Navy had been to this beach before. Fences had been put up to keep us from straying too far into the island. I remember looking past the fences into small village areas nestled in trees. It looked as though the villagers were living in tree houses. All of this brought back memories of the hand held slide viewers in the Akron Public Library. Earlier days in looking through them had introduced me to scenes such as I was now viewing in person.

Natives of the island knew by this time that a liberty party on their island meant cash business. The natives, dressed in what I thought was very little, approached the fence with their wares. I purchased a bolo knife that I still have among my prized souvenirs. I was afraid to eat the food items they offered to sell us. We had been rehearsed earlier to tell them, "no thank you."

I would hear some of my shipmates really carry on with the young girls that came to the fence. I knew what my shipmates wanted, but also knew they could not get to the young girls to satisfy their physical desires. Both men and women natives could be seen taking care of nature's need for the elimination of body waste. It did not seem to matter to them where they were standing or who was watching. The culture I grew up with in America's heartland had been challenged by customs that the Navy had abruptly flung my way. Now I had to witness another style of life that caused me to record in my memory that the world is very large  and my world back home was but a very small part.

On another day, the Skipper decided we needed more land duty.  Each time we would go ashore, beer and cokes would be provided.  They were just tossed in piles on the sand.  We could have two bottles each of beer and coke.   My beer always went to one of my buddies that wanted it.  I always kept my Navy issued knife hooked to my belt.  Some of my shipmates did not think to do this and would come up to me and say, "Shrout, I need to use your bottle opener." They would pop open the hot bottle of beer and it would spew all over me.  I did not like that too much and hated the smell of it.  But, anything for a shipmate.

On some of the beach trips, we would get into a game of softball.  I ended up being the pitcher most of the time.  I noticed that the extended time spent aboard ship had a price tag, for  much of the hard readiness that boot camp had provided our soft civilian bodies, now showed signs of diminishing.   My legs and arms ached each evening when we returned back aboard ship.  But this was exactly what the Navy wanted; we needed the exercise.

**Phillipine bum boats selling their "wares"**

# SHROUT - AFTER the MUD

As soon as the natives learned where we were anchored they began to pay us visits. They paddled out to see us in homemade dugouts with floats on each side for stability. A common item to peddle were bananas. Fresh fruit hit the spot if you were not afraid to eat it.

Another popular commodity was sex. The native men would paddle out after dark, bringing with them either their sisters, or in some cases, it could have been their wives. I was told by participants that there would be a line up on the fantail of the **73**, each waiting with their two dollars in hand for a chance at the merchandise. I was also told that after each sale the woman would dip her hand into the sea and swish salt water over the used area; whereupon the native male would whisper eagerly, "Next." This was too much for my upbringing. I avoided the fantail when I heard activity was happening there. If I knew this activity was occurring, surely the Captain was also aware. I wondered what he thought about this indulgence.

My memories of this laid back society of the Philippines have followed me through life. It does not matter how much of an environment of simple living habits we come from, there will always be someplace where living is more simple. Even my life on the Shewman farm in Indiana was starting to look progressive. We did at least have outhouses.

# 8.

# JAPAN - HERE WE COME

## Peace and Occupation

September 17, 1945, saw us securing anchor at 0832 and moving out of San Pedro Bay, Leyte. The war was over. Japan's surrender had taken place aboard the battleship *USS Missouri*. The R&R (rest and recreation) had been scheduled for us so that we would be in tip top shape to make the invasion of Japan. The **73** was part of a group proposed to storm the beaches of Tokyo Harbor. Thank God, the war was over and our trip north this Monday morning was to serve as occupation forces of Japan and help return this world to a state of peace.

We headed almost due North for four days and found ourselves heading into the same Buckner Bay of Okinawa we had been in just a little over a month ago. Four days later, Saturday, September 22, 1945, general quarters was sounded at 1300, for what turned out to be the last time for us. The last battle station was assumed and secured in 12 minutes and we were out of Buckner Bay and on our way to Kyushu, Japan.

It seemed such a short trip through the waters of our defeated enemy. Never in all of those weary days and nights of getting up and down for battle stations while at Okinawa, did I realize just how close we were to the mainland of Japan. While passing the harbor of Nagasaki, we were told that atom bomb number two had been unleashed with the fury of which could only be likened unto what it must be like in hell. Nagasaki had been laid to waste just a short time before our presence, on August 9, 1945.

As I looked across the span of water that separated our ship and the ruins of what once was a live city, pangs of pity ran through my mind. This was horrible! But it did put an end to the world's worst era of destroying human life. History has since told us that many more hundreds of thousands of lives would have been sacrificed had there been an all out invasion. My life and the lives of my shipmates would have probably been among them.

**Sasebo, Japan**
**A surrendered Japanese destroyer in the foreground**

Sasebo Ko Harbor, Kyushu, Japan, was our destination. We passed through the harbor entrance at 1600, Monday, September 24, 1945. All of the Japanese ships seemed to be ready for us. Not in the way they would have been had it been another situation of war, but today they had all of their men on deck, standing at attention as we passed by. I knew they did not know just what to expect-- maybe death!

We dropped anchor very close to shore. I could see some activity on the docks as an occasional worker would move something around. We were at last on the enemy's home ground. I could see several steep hills rising up behind the docks. There was some indication of small housing scattered on the hillsides. This was Japan, and we had come very close to destroying many of its cities. My thoughts flashed back to what Nagasaki looked and smelled like just a few short hours before. We must have had more than just two of these atomic bombs. I am so thankful we did not have to use any more.

During the first couple days in Japan we did very little. We moved about from one supply ship to another replenishing our various inventories. I spent a great deal of time watching the shoreline, hoping to see some activity. I wondered what the people of Sasebo were thinking as they looked out in the harbor and saw the American flags flying.

I had a better opportunity to check the attitudes and faces of the Japanese on our fifth day in Japan. We were formed into small groups of six, with one assigned to carry a loaded side piece. We took turns catching a liberty launch that was moving about the harbor from ship to ship. The launch deposited us on shore and we were ready to do our first occupying. I really did not know what to expect. I tried to imagine how I would have felt if the situation had been reversed.

The group I was with started walking up through the buildings that rimmed the wharf. As we moved deeper into the residential area we came into what seemed to be a small group of retail stores. I remember I attempted to purchase something, only I did not know how much to pay for the item to which I had pointed. We had been instructed to use our American dollars. The clerk that waited upon me was really scared. I could tell. He nervously gave me the package I had chosen (it looked like some kind of cookie) and started pushing Japanese yen back to me in exchange for my American dollar bill. I nodded my approval and scooped up the change and left the small store.

Next I attempted to get change in what I am sure was a bank. The clerk that was at the counter seemed to have more knowledge about money exchange. He checked some type of a chart and counted out in his native tongue the change for my American bill. I was starting to get the hang of it. My only problem was that I did not know what they were saying to me.

Our small liberty party moved up into the hills, winding around on the small crooked roads with houses that were strange looking to me. Frequently, an occupant would come out of his house, bow and greet us in some fashion. All of this special attention was extremely interesting to me. I must say, I believe we did a good job of occupying. We smiled back, nodded our heads and proceeded up the road. I recall that a couple of our guys had learned the word for whiskey in Japanese and kept asking for it from the people we encountered on our walking trip. No success. We also asked the people we met if they had any Japanese flags we could have or purchase. No luck there, either.

We went back to our ship on the same launch. As I sat around the rest of the evening, writing to those back home about where I had been, I remember telling them the people we met were not scary, but were friendly. I was so glad the war was over and we did not have to go ashore and do injury to kind looking people, such as the ones we saw that day in Sasebo.

On another trip, I had the experience of using a common restroom where men and women came and went as though there was nothing to hide.  That was a culture shock for me!  We also visited a large warehouse and selected our own personal Japanese rifle, complete with bayonet, for our war souvenir.

We began harbor entry duty--the Navy called it our "Harbor Entrance Control Post."  Our ship anchored at the entry to Sasebo Harbor and accepted surrender of Japanese ships.  They had been ordered to return to the nearest port and turn themselves in.  What a sight!  They would have all of their personnel on deck, full uniform and standing at attention as they slowly moved through the harbor entrance.  I just knew they thought this was going to be a massacre for them.

Three Japanese harbor pilots at a time would come to our ship, via a small boat, spend the day and give directions to the captains of the surrendering ships as they, one by one, reported in.  All of this activity is still implanted deep in my memory and brings to my conscience pictorial evidences of the conclusion of World War II.

**Sasebo, Japan**
**A surrendered Japanese Cruiser awaiting our orders**

**Lt. Carlton and Ensign Spencer (back row) posing with three Japanese harbor pilots**

# SHROUT - AFTER the MUD

My nineteenth birthday will always be remembered. As the day of October tenth progressed, the winds grew heavier and the sea more violent. We received word aboard ship that a typhoon was on the way. The name, Louise, was given to it, even before it hit with its hardest force. At 1440, a three inch bow line parted during winds gusting to 90 knots. All hands were summoned on deck to save the ship. The engine room had engines running and ready in case we were cast adrift. They were secured at 1750. The worst winds had receded.

As I relieved the midnight watch, fifteen minutes early as usual, I remember that Spear, the ship's baker, had made a fresh chocolate sheet cake and gave me a piece to celebrate my nineteenth birthday. I ate this piece of goodness as I watched the clock reach and pass into the official day of October 11, 1945.

The next several days saw some of my older shipmates leaving the **73** for the states and ultimate honorable discharge. The war was over and there was no point in keeping the married men, and particularly the fathers, away from their loved ones any longer. It was time for them to go home and reap the rewards of many months of service to their country.

Several times, we moved about in the harbor and tied alongside some of the Japanese ships. I recall one late morning when we were next to one of their destroyers. Right out on the open deck, a large black pot with an open fire under it was boiling away with something cooking that smelled terrible, or at least to me it smelled uneatable. The crew would come by, one by one, dip a community ladle into the steaming pot, sip and make signs that they approved of its taste. It looked like it contained turnips or some other root product that did not appeal to my liking.

**Occupation of Sasebo, Japan**
**The author is aboard the *USS LCS(L)(3)73***

268

# 9.

# HOMEWARD BOUND

## Good News

October slowly moved to a completion and I was beginning to wonder just how long we would stay in Sasebo. I did not have to wait long into the month of November. It was Monday, November 5, 1945. At 0914 I left ship for my journey back to America and to my beloved Indiana. I had finally been granted an emergency leave to return home. My mother had died the previous July and it had taken the Navy four months to catch up.

A small launch delivered me and my shipmates to the Sasebo dock. Navy personnel met us and dispatched us to different ships by more Navy launches. I was sent to the *AKA 15*. This was a cargo ship that had several cargo holes, each with a removable wooden cover. The ship was being used to transport troops back to the states. I was issued a folding cot and a space assigned on one of the

269

hole covers. All of this was another new experience for me. This ship was extremely large compared to the **73**. One could get lost on it very easily.

The next day, November 6, 1945, the *AKA 15* pulled anchor and headed out of Sasebo harbor for America. Was I ever happy! When we came around the southern tip of Japan we set a northeasterly course and headed for the Aleutian Islands, some two thousand plus miles away. It may seem strange, but a straight line on the surface of the earth is not necessarily the shortest distance from one point to another. By going slightly north towards the Aleutians we would save many miles in reaching our destination, Seattle, Washington. Looking around a globe can bring one to agree with this theory.

The closer we came to the Aleutians, the colder it became. There seemed to be no heat available in the cargo holes. We spent our time during the day up on topside. Even the open-aired deck felt warmer. At night, our cots would slide around on ice that had formed on the deck cover, and our cots would bump into each other. We didn't get much sleep in this situation. But little was said; we all were heading home and that was what really counted.

The Navy personnel in Seattle quickly moved my papers through all of the red tape, and I found myself in a railroad passenger car headed for Chicago that first evening out of Seattle. I was given a 30 day leave. I arrived home in Indiana in time to spend Thanksgiving with Dad and the rest of my family. It seemed so strange not to be greeted by my mother. When I arrived home, I looked across the lawn from the driveway towards the house. I could easily see into the kitchen window. This was the same window that I had pictured in my mind so many times while aboard the **73**, with the image of my mother as she often looked out. She was not there. And that was very difficult for me to deal with.

With family and close friends to visit and good food to eat, the thirty days of leave slipped by quickly. I returned to Warsaw, caught a train to Chicago and on to San Francisco. My orders were to report to Camp Shoemaker, a Navy receiving point for reassigning sailors to ships and other points of duty. I remember the camp being so busy and so overcrowded that after we ate in the chow hall, we would often get right back in the chow line again to be ready for the next meal. The line never ended.

**The author with the Golden Gate Bridge in background**

I was given a temporary assignment of patrol duty in San Francisco Bay. Three of us made up the crew of a small thirty-two foot picket boat. Our assignment was to stand by at pier thirty-five, using a small sleeping quarters, but be ready day or night to run out into the bay and give anchoring directions to any incoming Navy ship loaded with returning servicemen. This proved to be interesting, and I enjoyed the assignment. When not on duty I stayed on Treasure Island. The Navy had taken over the island that still had many World's Fair buildings remaining. Our barracks was very nice. The fact that the buildings were made for the fair perhaps was the reason.

I rode a water taxi from Treasure Island over to San Francisco. Liberties were given often, and I participated in as many as I was offered. Lodging was scarce, but I managed to get some pretty nice accommodations and spent several evenings away from the base on Treasure Island.

While I was home on the thirty day leave, I had filed a petition for discharge from the Navy, listing hardship conditions in my father's case. One day in February my name was called over the loud speaker, and I was on my way to start the discharge proceedings the same day. It was over! Good-bye, Navy! I headed for my beloved Indiana, February 21, 1946.

**Reunion of the 73 in Florida, 1997**
**Seven of the crew - from left to right**

**Wunder,Weber,Shrout,Morris,Lemke,Ellenberger,Little**

# EPILOGUE

It is fascinating to watch the waves of the mighty Pacific churn into white soapy looking lather as it washes against the Oregon coast. In nature's display of its unusual strength,   small bubbles are created that disappear into the many sands of the water's edge.

As I look backward in time today, I can liken what I see from my motel room to those episodes of my past. I can see beyond the horizon even though it might be obscured with the overcast of the day.  One of the greatest gifts my Creator has allowed me to receive and  to retain throughout my many years of life, is my memory.   How detailed and precious is this heavenly endowment.   I am eternally grateful for this special gift.

I can almost see the silhouette of the **73**, my ship of war, as it moved south along this very coast exactly fifty five years ago of this chronicalization.   More than half a century has slid into history since that memorable voyage. In spite of what my calendar reveals to me, much of what happened during World War ll seems to have occurred only yesterday. To a young man fresh from America's rural heartland, Uncle Sam's Navy was truly another world. I had matured into early adulthood, minus many of the experiences my city shipmates had in experimenting with life.

Life in the 1940s in a small rural farming community provided the basics of how to exist in a society free of fear. Neighbor looked after neighbor. Houses, in many cases, did not have working locks. Those that had them were, for the most part, not put to use. Not many threats were made that proved really dangerous. The local official keeper of the law did not wear a gun. I did not hear of a shot being fired in defense of our serenity while I was a resident of the Akron community.

From the clutches of such a society, a young, naive farm lad was thrust into the world to become a warrior for democracy. I sincerely felt the instruction received from my parents had been endorsed as the norm of my community. During this time in America, double standards in what is recognized as proper now, were then non-existent. I hardly knew what the word prejudice meant, let alone use it or practice its characteristics. I quickly recognized the value of the fundamentals my parents and my community had instilled within me. I found that it was not difficult for me to exist in any of my naval assignments, because of those simple basics I had latched onto either at my parent's knee or from those experiences of my church, school, and community.

The world at war presented a need for America to be united in a fervent spirit not known before in the pages of our history. America has always responded to whatever situation was thrust before her. Never had this need been so demanding and challenging as the aftermath created on that day, December 7, 1941, at Pearl Harbor.

World War ll managed to create many new positions of employment for a country freshly emerging from a time when many were hungry for a job. The Great Depression had swept across America with an unrelentless fervor of devastation. One would often hear the corner conversations move from the rewards of their having work, to what was happening on the battle fronts.

Patriotism ran rampant throughout America. Uncle Sam's face and pointing finger graced almost every street corner all across the nation. "Uncle Sam needs you," the sign would inform us as we walked by. If you were not quite seventeen, you could hardly wait to become old enough to enlist in your country's service. If you were too old or not physically qualified, you were perhaps content to be working alongside a "Rosie the riveter."

As I look out across the Pacific, my mind ponders an interesting scenario. When I gaze across the water, I am looking west. In the Phillipine Islands, Okinawa, and even in Japan, the inhabitants look across the Pacific in an easterly direction. Back and forth over the decades, the tides of time have chased this huge body of water. Small glass floats pitch and toss for years and finally make it to the Pacific shore. Today as I watch the water slither upon the sand of America's coast, I wonder what piece of time might it contain?

I can still see the star shells that lit the brush that contained men of war on the beaches of Okinawa. Men of two nations, all determined to fight to death if necessary to protect the honor of their country. I think of the Japanese soldiers who attempted to reach freedom from certain death on land by jumping into the sea. Here their fate was placed in our hands as the **73** and other such ships blew them out of the water and into eternity. I think that the Japanese, also, must have coveted freedom and peace. Americans, for the most part, wanted to exist in peace and tranquility in whatever situation, be it the big city or small hamlet.

I have also contemplated many times the positive results fate  might have dealt to me in my assignment to the amphibious part of the Navy. Submarine duty, as I had requested, could have had another ending for me.

Perhaps if that had happened, I would not be here writing this chronicle. I will never know. I like to think that God had his hand in all of this and wanted me to touch some of His future precious creations: namely, my children.

During the many battles, staged on both land and sea, there was much blood shed that spilled into the sands and water of the Pacific. Is it possible that some twenty thousand plus days later, more than five decades, a small isolated particle of this sacrifice is still intact? If so, and as it churns about, could it not deposit itself on American soil? Many American servicemen gave their lives to make a statement; a statement of their ownership of freedom and truth.

Those that drafted the document of surrender and ultimately world peace, did not have in mind the political and social struggles over pro-life, pro-choice, alternative lifestyles and the need to always be politically correct. I also believe the American serviceman that paid the ultimate sacrifice did not concern himself about such issues. I am apprehensive that decades after Pearl Harbor we are engrossed in debates that could be destroying our very democracy for which we fought and died.

This author returned to his small hamlet when discharged. In those first days, as I would sit on a three-legged milk stool, milking one of Dad's cows, I remember thinking, is this what it was all for? Life seemed so simple. You cut the hay in the field. You put the hay in a manager. The cow comes into the barn and eats the hay. The cow digests the hay and makes milk. And here I was, pulling the cow's teats and aiming good wholesome milk into the milk bucket. Why would mankind want to unbalance a balanced plan of living like this?

After all these many years, those of us who remain and who have attempted to demonstrate the defending of our country's honor, still prefer freedom and peace. The tides of time that beat upon the shores of America help register this affirmation more vividly. In fact, it fuels the act of our determination to continue to defend our choices.